A DOG'S WAY

How Dogs Make Us Better People

Dean Miller

www.thedogcounselor.com

ISBN: 1502598272
ISBN 13: 9781502598271
Library of Congress Control Number: 2014917909
CreateSpace Independent Publishing Platform
North Charleston, South Carolina

TABLE OF CONTENTS

To all the dogs I've known,
who have taught me so much
about myself, life and how to love.

FORWARD

After years of studying dogs and their behavior, the way that they think and communicate makes perfect sense to me. Their logic is simple and straightforward. They make decisions in the blink of an eye, react out of pure instinct and communicate volumes to each other without saying a single word.

They can't do math or drive a car or write a novel or bake a pie. However, in countless other areas, they have vast capabilities that we have only barely begun to understand. I have absolute respect for them and I hope that more people will take a moment to appreciate who they are, what they have to offer and the great teachers they can be.

They are little miracles and beautiful gifts. They teach us just as much about ourselves as we teach them, in return. Through give and take, trial and error, love and empathy, we begin to see ourselves reflected in their eyes. They are perfect little mirrors of insight into our souls. Without a word, they can open a whole new world to us, if we are open to the possibility.

"He is my other eyes that can see above the clouds; my other ears that hear above the winds. He is the part of me that can reach out into the sea. He has told me a thousand times over that I am his reason for being; by the way he rests against my leg; by the way he thumps his tail at my smallest smile; by the way he shows his hurt when I leave without taking him. (I think it makes him sick with worry when he is not along to care for me.) When I am wrong, he is delighted to forgive. When I am angry, he clowns to make me smile. When I am happy, he is joy unbounded. When I am a fool, he ignores it. When I succeed, he brags. Without him, I am only another man. With him, I am all-powerful. He is loyalty itself. He has taught me the meaning of devotion. With him, I know a secret comfort and a private peace. He has brought me understanding where before I was ignorant. His head on my knee can heal my human hurts. His presence by my side is protection against my fears of dark and unknown things. He has promised to wait for me... whenever... wherever - in case I need him. And I expect I will - as I always have. He is just my dog."
- Gene Hill, *Tears and Laughter*

DOG LOVE

The way a dog loves has taught me an infinite number of lessons about life. Through a lifetime of relationships with a large number of very special dogs, I have learned a beautiful way of moving through the world. Dogs have taught me how to simplify. Life is so much easier when we get to the point and cut out all of the extraneous stuff that simply doesn't matter.

I have learned how to get to the point. After watching dogs communicate paragraphs of information with a look or a body posture, I have applied that to my every day human interactions.

I have learned how to love unconditionally. I don't base my giving of love on how much I am given in return. I don't withhold my feelings just because someone else is withholding theirs. If I am being mistreated, it doesn't mean I have to sink to that level and mistreat someone in return. I can always stay true to who I am. I don't have to be negatively changed by the circumstances around me.

I have learned to stand my ground when I know I'm right. Often, I don't have to argue, struggle or even speak. I can just quietly hold my position until the other person lets go of their position. I learned this from dogs.

I have learned how to effectively use the sound of my voice in a confident, powerful way without being bossy or controlling. I can simply speak confidently and concisely. I don't beat around the bush. I don't have to explain myself with a thousand extra words. I can simply "be" and others infer the kind of person I am by the way I am holding myself and the voice I am using.

I have learned that I don't have to do anything to be loved. I love my dogs simply because they are who they are. They don't have to do anything to earn my love. They are deserving of love just by existing. I have learned that if I can love them the way they are, having done nothing to elicit this love, then I can be loved that way, too.

I have learned that a picture is worth a thousand words. I now listen less to what people are telling me with their words and look more into what they are showing me between and behind the words. A person's eyes, body language, behavior and voice all tell me the truth of what they are about. This is one of the most beautiful lessons dogs have taught me.

I encourage you to take the time to sit still and watch some dogs. Go to the park, visit a neighbor, go to a shelter. Find a group of dogs and watch them interact. You will begin to tune into a world of communication, which transcends our way of communicating. If you watch long enough, so many beautiful, simple social ways will become clear.

Dogs have a way of distilling life down to its most important moments. They are clear and unwavering in their direct means of communicating. If we could learn to tap into this beautiful, loving, spiritual way of interacting, I believe we would all be better for it. I think peace and serenity are not things we find outside of ourselves. They come from the inside out.

If anyone can lead us in this direction, it's a dog. He doesn't have the complexity of mind to get in his own way. He simply lives and reacts. He starts from a foundation of love and trust. He gives unconditionally. He says what he means and means what he says. He is a great teacher while being an incredible student. He reflects the best in us by giving the best of himself.

This is why I love dogs.

TREAT ME LIKE A DOG

Every time I hear someone say that, I think, "I would love to be treated the way I treat my dog!" Even more so, I'd love to be treated the way dogs treat others!

Most dogs I know are honest, loyal, trusting, eager to please. They give of themselves and above all else, love unconditionally. They are faithful, direct, communicate simply and are incapable of lying.

"You don't know *my* dog!"

I hear that all the time. It may be true that I've never met your particular dog, but I've met thousands of dogs in my life. I've worked with hundreds of tough cases and some problems that seemed unsolvable. While every dog is an individual and no two dogs are exactly alike, all dogs have certain wonderful, incredible traits in common. So, without ever having met your dog, I already know a lot about him... even if I've never seen him before in my life!

I know, for example, that he does not think the same way you and I do. He may learn to live in our world, adapt to our way of doing things and even grow to love our way of life. However, somewhere deep inside him, he will always be a dog. That means if we learn to fulfill that "dogness" deep inside him, we can help him to feel balanced, happy, confident and content.

Every dog is different in many ways, as well. Each one is an individual with his or her own unique personality. In fact, it always strikes me as funny that we say "PERSON-ality" about a dog. Shouldn't we be saying "DOG-anality"? He's not a person at all and he never will be. Your dog is a unique individual with his own habits, traits, likes and dislikes. He has his own feelings and emotions, his own wants and desires. But he is not a person.

All dogs have a lot in common. They are all pack animals, inspired to follow a pack order and a pack mentality. They have a "family" approach to handling things. They look for structure, order and, above all else, an alpha dog. They want to know there is an authority figure in each pack that inspires trust and loyalty. Dogs crave an alpha dog to lead and inspire them. I am NOT talking about force. I do NOT mean control. They do NOT want to be intimidated. A dog wants to be inspired!

You can't make a dog like you. You can pour on love, treats, beg, bribe and plead to try and win him over. But no matter what you do, you can't force your dog to like you. It will always be his choice.

The good news is you can *inspire* him to love you!

The chances are he will choose to love you, anyway, no matter what you do. You don't really have to do anything to achieve that. He will simply make the decision on his own. That means you have inspired him to love you just by being you!

Isn't that beautiful?

Have you ever tried to make a person like you? You dress differently, act differently and pour on the compliments. You try to get their attention, say what you think they want to hear, try to be like them. None of it works. The fact is, you are trying to force something to happen that just won't happen at all and it's making you crazy! You start making yourself unhappy simply because you can't make that person like you.

Isn't that ridiculous?

One of the wonderful things about dogs is that they don't judge us the same way we judge each other. They use an entirely different set of criteria. We make decisions about people all the time. We base our judgments on looks, experience, education, wealth, attitude, appearance, words and thousands more indicators. We rely on these things to tell us what we should think about a person. These snap judgments help us decide how we will end up treating a person. Are they pretty, educated, rich or well spoken? Are they scowling, mean, dirty or disheveled?

Dogs don't care about any of those things! Dogs base their judgments on the person we are. They only care about who we present ourselves to be from the inside out. For example, one way a dog will "size you up" is according to smell. They can tell some of the places you've been, with whom you've had contact and even whether or not you're wearing deodorant! They don't care so much whether or not you've had a bath or brushed your teeth. They can, however, sense your fear, insecurity, confidence, calm and sometimes even your health. They have trained dogs to detect cancer in the human body, predict seizures and even tell a diabetic when their insulin levels drop. They can hear so much more in your voice than just what you are saying. In fact, they are always paying more attention to the way you are saying something rather than the words you are using.

Their acute sensitivity is a miracle!

If you tell a dog to do something, but he can tell that you don't mean it, he is more likely to listen to the "true" part of you that doesn't mean it or isn't in control. In other words, your dog is paying less attention to the words you're saying or the front you are putting forward. He doesn't care about the mask you put on for the world. He is far more interested in your state of mind and what you are feeling at your core. He is responding to the truth of who you really are in the moment. He is paying attention to the real you.

I think this is one of the biggest reasons we love dogs so much. This "truth meter" cuts through the social rules and inhibitions we might have with people and get to the heart of who we truly are. They are not capable of lying. They are not capable of faking friendship and loyalty. They can't show you one thing and then turn around and be something completely different. They are who they are.

What you see is what you get. If a dog doesn't like you, he simply doesn't like you. If a dog seems afraid, he is afraid. Many times it's because he just doesn't trust you. Maybe he's had some terrible experiences in his past. Sometimes he may have no real reason at all. We all have people we like and dislike. But to a dog, he never makes his decision based on the way you are dressed, the car you drive or if you are wearing the right designer labels!

A dog will never show affection if he isn't "feeling it". He will never pretend to be your friend and then turn around and stab you in the back. He'll never lie, he'll never deceive you and he'll never say one thing and mean another.

He simply can't.

I have been working with dogs for many years and as a child, I spent many years just being with dogs, living with them and observing. They have made me so much more aware of who I am and what I am all about. I feel so strongly about this that I wanted to share my experiences with everybody else.

That is why I wrote this book.

Whether loving us unconditionally, sacrificing themselves for the good of someone else or even times when they show their fear and blind rage, I love dogs anyway. There is always a beauty, a story, a poignant sadness or a lesson beneath the face they present. My hope is to help others appreciate them in the same way I do and pass on the gift they have given to me thousands of times over.

DOG LOGIC

I once worked with a dog named Zeke, who came from the home of a dog hoarder who kept hundreds of dogs in a very small house.

The person had intended to care for his dogs but had become overwhelmed. They couldn't keep up with the feeding, the care, the cleaning and the attention each dog required. The house had become a nightmare of noise and waste, smell and overcrowding.

On top of this toxic environment, Zeke had been removed from his mother and littermates too early and, therefore, had not learned many of the crucial things a dog needs to learn in the early days of his life. He lived in an overcrowded, filthy home with no guidance whatsoever. Any human interaction he had was limited and he never saw the outside, grass or sunshine.

Zeke's home had been raided by the authorities and the dogs had been confiscated. They were put up for adoption in many different places. Zeke's new owner called me and asked if I would come and help with his adjustment to a new way of living. His social skills needed a lot of work and he was terrified of everything, to the point of completely shutting down.

Most human beings facing a situation like this see love as the only answer. Of course, it's gut wrenching to see a dog so damaged by another person. We get angry, upset and feel sorry for the dog. That's only natural. We pour on the love and treats and try to gain the dog's trust and confidence through endless affection. However, the dog is stuck in a terrible state of mind. He really needs a different kind of solution to his problems.

He needs someone with enough patience and understanding to know that a dog's needs in this kind of situation are very different than those of a human.

If you saw a person drowning in a swimming pool, what would you do? You would pull them out of the water and get that person to safety, right?

The last thing they would want you to do is jump in the water with them and say how sorry you feel for them. A drowning person doesn't need a hug at that moment. He doesn't need to hear all of your reassurances that everything will be okay. He needs a strong person to grab him and lead him out of his dire situation. He wants to be rescued. He wants to feel protected by something stronger than he is. You can love him, later. For now, save him! That's exactly what a dog like this needs.

Think of it this way.

Your dog is "drowning". He is a convoluted mess of fears, sadness, mistrust and zero guidance. He has no coping skills. He has no experience in a human home with gentle guidance and teaching that he should have received at an early age. He has had to learn that in order to survive, he could not count on anyone else. He has been let down time and again. He has learned that when you trust others, they always fail you. He has had to become his own leader. Whether he was equipped for the job or not, a dog like this has got to survive. His past is filled with people who let him down.

What a dog like this needs, more than anything else in the world, is leadership. He needs a rock to lean on. He needs to know that there is someone on his side looking out for his best interests. He needs someone to protect him. He needs a leader, an alpha figure to stand up for him. Otherwise, he can't find a way to get past his neurosis and learn to trust.

A dog's instinct is to rely on a pack leader. He doesn't pick his leader based on who is the sweetest and has the most treats. That may make you his best friend. Of course he's going to love you for that. But when it comes to leadership, he wants to follow someone strong.

He wants to turn over his own, personal authority to someone better qualified to handle the role. He is most likely to follow and trust someone who has just the right balance of strength and kindness, leadership and calm self-assurance. He looks for someone who is firm, but fair, strong, but loving.

Even the most damaged dog wants to know first and foremost that you are equipped to protect him. He wants to know that you have yourself together more than he does. He knows he's got problems. He wants to know that you have fewer problems than he does and that you have a plan to get him out of this. Prove that you have the strength to protect him, along with the loving kindness to never use that strength against him, and he will be devoted to you for life!

When I first met Zeke, he was a fearful mess. From the moment I entered the house, he ran into a corner or under a table to find safety. He only felt secure under something, far from anyone's reach. In moments like these, most people feel the need to start speaking lovingly to the dog. "It's okay! You're okay, puppy! Come here! Poor baby!"

The irony of this approach is that things are NOT okay. He is terrified! Nothing has been okay for most of his life. Now, here we are reaching for him, speaking in weird voices he's never heard and chasing him all over the place.

He has already told you he wants nothing to do with you. He's already shown you he wants you to stay away. Forcing yourself on him with touching and petting and loud sounds are all overwhelming and intimidating. You're showing him that you don't respect his personal space. Plus, the sound of, "It's okay! You're okay!" is said with the same tone of voice as, "Good boy!" To him, the tone is more meaningful than the word. So, to him, it sounds just like, "Good boy! Nice job!" In other words, he is interpreting this as praise for being so fearful!

In a situation like this, I suggest making no sound at all. With Zeke, I approached him as closely as he would let me without bolting. I may even have him in a corner, so he doesn't run away. But I only approach him close enough as to not shut him down or have him try to leave. I turn my side or my back to him, I make no eye contact, no sound and I sit on the ground. I want it to appear that I am absolutely no threat to him and he can approach me at his own pace. He can reach out to me in his own time, at his own comfort level, if at all. I will not force myself into his space.

Have you ever been afraid of someone? Imagine if that person began speaking in a high-pitched voice and reaching for your neck (collar) and forcing you closer and closer.

Would that make you feel safe and secure?

Of course not!

What if they turned slightly away and remained indifferent toward you?

What if they spoke in calm tones, or not at all, looking away from you?

What if they faced the opposite direction protecting you from whatever might be coming to get you?

Would that help you relax and assess the situation?

Zeke began sniffing in my direction, checking me out in his own time. Gradually, he allowed me to loop a leash around his neck, again, with no sound. Once I'd accomplished this, I brought him closer to me. He started to flip and flop and resist, but I remained calm and quiet, always returning the leash to a loose, slack position with no tension. A step or two at a time, with rests in between and he gradually moved into my space. Before long, Zeke began to get tired and realized I wasn't hurting him. In fact, I was having no reaction at all to his behavior. I was neutral.

No one can throw a tantrum for very long. They realize it's having no effect and eventually they grow tired. In that moment, a dog will have a glimpse of clarity. I have controlled him, but nothing bad has happened to him. I have not used this control to hurt him. In fact, unbeknownst to him, he has freely given me his control. I have dominated him passively.

This is our first breakthrough to trust!

Zeke responded perfectly. He tried several times to take off. He pulled and threw a couple of short tantrums. I blocked his exit with the leash, using zero force, until he had no choice but to stay where he was. I always returned the leash to a slack, loose position when he calmed down. As his frantic behavior failed to produce the result he wanted, he gradually surrendered his control to me.

As I gained trust and authority over the situation, I moved a little closer to him. Little-by-little I reached my hand toward him. Throughout all of this, I was making little or no sound. Zeke was unable to run away, but able to discover me at his own pace.

I slowly got to the point where I could touch him without him trying to bolt. I didn't pet him or show affection. I simply rested my hand on him. I touched him with no agenda behind it. I touched him in a neutral way. I was not petting and praising with my voice. I was not escalating the situation. I was DE-escalating. If I had done any of this while he was in a panicked state of mind, he would have interpreted my praise as being rewarded for his neurotic behavior.

As I felt Zeke relax, I let my hand begin to pet him. Slowly, he began to associate my affection and attention with his ability to relax and turn over his leadership to me.

Exciting, isn't it?

He earns praise from his strong, but fair, new pack leader. He learns to trust first and be loved second. He gives his authority to a figure stronger than he is, so he feels safe and protected. This pack leader uses that trust to keep the dog safe and secure. Once this is established, the leader can now, gradually, show affection. This is the natural order of things for dogs and Zeke blossomed in response.

None of this was accomplished through human conversation. Words had nothing to do with it. You can't have a wordy, verbal conversation with a dog and expect him to reason through your complex wants and desires for him. However, if you proceed with patience, calm and "dog logic" you can see results almost immediately. You just have to do it the way dogs do it, not the way people do.

I can't tell you that Zeke was completely cured in minutes. However, by the end of an hour with him, he was able to nap near me, he would come toward me, share affection, friendship and he lost his desire to run away.

Over time with his adoptive Dad, he has blossomed into a confident, healthy, happy little dog. He was not led out of his sad state of mind by overwhelming baby talk, treats and affection. He was led by strength, calm and loving balance.

Often, we try to control a situation by forcing an issue. We want the dog to sit in our lap and receive petting and affection. So, we reach for them, grab them, talk a lot and try to make them understand our crazy human desires. What I've learned from dogs is that the solution often lies in quiet patience. There is a great feeling in allowing something to happen in its own time.

I always tell people... 'Don't try to teach your dog when you are in a hurry. Don't try to rush progress. Don't try to make him learn, especially when you are in a stressful moment or a frustrated state of mind. Don't push your agenda onto your dog.'

Use gentle, calm and inspiring ways of presenting yourself. It will go much farther than force and control. This is not only true of dogs but people, as well.

A DOG IS NOT A PERSON

A lot of us don't like to admit it, but there is a fundamental trait that is common to every, single dog.

They are dogs. They are not human.

Nobody loves their dogs any more than I do and I must admit, there are times I "humanize" my dog as much as, or maybe even more than, the next person. Luckily, my dogs have lived with me long enough to forgive me for this. I think they realize my baby talk and affectionate gestures are as much about fulfilling my needs as theirs. However, they are animals. I know that and I accept that. I suppose I just forget sometimes.

On the other hand, we're animals, too. We're just a different species. If we learn to accept this and honor our differences, we can actually deepen our relationship and strengthen our bond with our dogs.

When it comes to making decisions, dogs have a completely different kind of logic than we do. They don't face a problem with any kind of human reasoning. They react from a place of instinct rather than a thought out process of reason.

Dogs work very hard to understanding us. They spend all day observing, calculating, absorbing and reading our actions, our sounds and our movements. They try to "get" what it is we're about. They want to know what makes us tick and how to best live in our world.

Unfortunately, we don't always return the favor. A lot of us tend to adopt a dog, turn him loose in our home and hope for the best. We don't take the time to slowly acclimate him to our environment. We don't always teach him patiently what is expected of him. We need to slowly learn about his feelings and supply his needs.

I can't tell you how many people I have encountered who take a dog into their family only to be amazed and frustrated when he begins acting like a dog!

"Why is my dog chewing everything in sight?"

Because he is a dog!

"Why is my dog urinating on everything?"

Because he is a dog!

"Why does my dog jump on me, bark and run around like crazy?"

Because he is a dog!

When your dog is housebroken, holds his urine, doesn't bark, doesn't jump up on you, doesn't chew and is generally polite, he is actually denying every instinct God instilled in him to follow. In other words, he is denying his own fundamental nature...for you!

He may be willing to do this for a number of reasons, but the reason I like most is simple. A dog is happiest when he is making the leader he loves happy! He makes these choices because he loves you.

How many animals do you know that will go against their nature just to make you happy? Would you do that for somebody else? This is one of the biggest reasons dogs are such a beautiful miracle.

LEADERSHIP

At the core of a dog's love for us is a fundamental principle. A dog wants to follow a self-assured, authoritative, calm and fair leader.

It is at the heart of every dog to respond to authoritative behavior from another animal. At this point, I always want to explain that authority is NOT the same as "mean". It is NOT the same as aggressive. We can show leadership and authority in a variety of ways without EVER being mean or harsh.

When a dog sits down and refuses to walk on the leash, he has just controlled you. It is what I call passive dominance. When a dog ignores your command and walks away, he has just dominated you. When he moves into your space and growls, he is behaving dominantly. But none of these behaviors are mean. A dog doesn't choose his behavior just to be mean. There is always a good reason behind it.

Deep in a dog's genetic history is a very strong survival instinct. This is one of the biggest reasons dogs are pack animals. There is safety in numbers. A group of dogs has a far better chance of survival in the wild than an individual dog. Predators have a lot less success attacking a pack of dogs than one, lone, weak straggler.

This "pack mentality" inspires a dog to seek out order, structure and, above all else, a leader. This leader sets the tone for behavior and obedience within the pack. He is the one who organizes life. He is the one who provides structure and security. Every dog pack needs a leader and every dog, deep down, wants to know who this leader is. This is who they instinctually want to follow.

The qualities a dog looks for in a leader are often quite different from those a human would look for. When we are children, we seek out loving, nurturing, gentle leaders. We want cuddling and warmth, food and gentleness. Dogs want this, too, but only after they find strong leadership. Love and affection are secondary desires after finding out "who's the boss".

Even as children, when humans are developing, we need a little bit of firm guidance and discipline. We crave structure and a disciplinary figure to lean on. As adults, we look to be treated politely and fairly. Yes, we respond to firm leadership, as well. But we are always looking for that to be tempered with respect.

Of course, a dog wants to be treated respectfully, too. He also needs love, nurturing and affection. However, his primary, primal need is to follow a leader that demonstrates calm strength and authority. A dog sees no reason to turn over his own authority to anyone unless they have shown him that they are better qualified to make decisions than he is. If this other dog (or person) shows himself to be more in control than he is, a dog will interpret this as strength. That means, if a bear or a wolf came crashing through the door, the more dominant creature is probably better equipped to handle the situation.

Why should your dog listen to you if you have caved in to his every wish or let slide his avoidance of your commands?

Why should he follow your orders if you can't even make him sit or stop digging in the trash or stealing your socks?

If your dog can get one over on you, then you certainly don't have the qualities he is looking for to lead him in dangerous situations. If he can control you in small ways, then, in his mind, you have no business controlling him at times that really matter.

The biggest difference between dogs and us, where this leadership is concerned, is the order in which this dominance is displayed. With dogs, authority comes first and love comes second. Dogs don't have time for politeness and beating around the bush. They need to know you are strong first and loving second. They need to know first and foremost that you will keep them safe. They want to know their survival is assured before they worry about sharing affection. They are more likely to put their trust in you once they feel you can protect them.

If you are in control, then you take a huge burden off of your dog's shoulders. If you're in charge, he no longer has to worry about guarding, protecting, barking, planning, herding and maintaining the order of the pack. All he has to do at that point is let go and follow you. He can relax. You can imagine how freeing this must seem to a dog!

Now, let's suppose something goes wrong.

This dog that we've adopted starts using our house as a toilet. Maybe he chews everything in sight or destroys out favorite possessions. This is usually the point we lose our patience, get frustrated and either begin yelling or, worse, hitting.

Terrible!

Think about it this way. Imagine you go to visit the home of someone in France. They have an entirely different language than yours. They come from a whole different culture and have their own set of customs, rules and ways of doing things. Let's imagine you go this person's home and start breaking the rules. First, they might ask you nicely to stop. Then they might tell you to go sit down. However, they're speaking French. You don't speak French. How are you supposed to understand what it is they want from you?

At this point, I would think this person, whose home this is, would become frustrated. They probably wouldn't like it that you are a guest in their home, violating their rules, acting disrespectfully and ignoring their pleas for you to stop. But you don't know any of these things. You have no idea what they're going on about. All you know is that someone is yelling at you in a foreign language, flailing their arms around and acting like a crazy person.

What if, after all of this agitation, this person reached out and hit you on the butt or popped you on the nose?

What if they started hitting you with a rolled up newspaper and chasing you through the house?

Then, let's say they grab you, rub your nose in some urine or feces and throw you outside.

How would that feel?

You would be no closer to understanding what's going on or what they want from you. You certainly wouldn't know any more of their language or what they are saying than you did when all of this began. It just doesn't make sense.

Why, then, do we adopt dogs and not bother to learn even a little bit of their language?

Why do we expect instant understanding of our expectations and miraculous results when we ask our dogs to do something?

Think of your dog as a foreigner. He has just stepped off the boat from another country, entering the U.S. for the first time. He doesn't know our customs or our culture. He doesn't know what to think about the way we live or the rules we follow. If you picture him in this way, your first steps of training will probably go a lot smoother and your relationship will blossom in a beautiful way.

As we have seen, dogs is that they are pack animals. They live in packs, roam in packs, and make decisions in packs, usually following the lead of a dominant pack leader. Whether you know it or not, you and your dog now live in a pack. Whether it's just the two of you living together, multiple dogs or other human family members, your dog sees this as his "pack". Within every pack, there must be a leader. An alpha dog.

The exception to this rule of leadership is the alpha dog. He is the born believing he is leader of the pack. This dog desires to lead, instead of being lead. He wants to dominate and not be dominated. He wants to tell you how things are and not vice versa. This "alpha dog" is the true leader of the pack, from the inside out. You can learn a lot by watching an alpha dog. His leadership is calm, quiet and peaceful. He has nothing to prove. He knows he's in control. He's usually pretty relaxed about his position. That's the way you should be. You need to be calm, relaxed and knowing you are the boss. It will show in the way you behave and affect the way your dog treats you. You need to become that alpha dog figure for your household, your family and your pack. Your dog will thank you for it!

Of course, this doesn't mean that if you have an alpha dog that he gets to be the leader of your house. It only means you might have to work a little bit harder before he relinquishes his control to you. From a very early age, an Alpha dog already believes he should be the boss. He has a kind of inner confidence and belief in himself many dogs don't have. You may really have to prove your leadership qualifications before he surrenders to you. However, once he does believe in you, just like all other dogs, he will adore you and follow as readily as any other dog. He just needs proof you are better at being boss than he is.

Fortunately, alpha dogs are a lot less common than follower dogs. Nature designed an amazing blueprint for the dog community at large. Only a very small percentage of dogs are born alphas. Nobody knows exactly why this is, but it is true. Submissive dogs far outweigh dominant dogs. The likelihood is that you already have a "follower" type of dog. Even if you don't, though, you can "out dominate" your dog with the right kind of language and technique, none of which involve cruelty or being loud or mean. You must become the alpha dog of your own pack.

The dog world has a miraculous order to it. Everybody knows his or her place in the pack. Once they know this place, the dogs in the pack tend to relax and surrender to the way things are. They are actually soothed by order, structure and knowing they are protected by an authoritative, calm, and fair leader. They don't resent being told what their place is. In fact, it comforts them.

MISUNDERSTANDING DOMINANCE

So many times, people have told me, "I don't want to be mean to my dog."

Of course not!

I don't want to be mean to my dogs, either!

Often, people hear the word "dominance" and immediately think that I mean "mean". Dominance, in the way I use the word, simply means having your will "dominate" your dog's will. This is accomplished every time you say, "sit" and your dog sits. Every time you ask him to move and he moves, you have just been dominant. It's should *never* be mean or harsh!

The word "dominant" is often misused when talking about dogs. There are too many trainers who go way overboard when it comes to the definition of this word. They think dominance has to mean tools and behaviors that physically dominate a dog into submission. I completely disagree with this approach. I believe in the least amount of correction necessary to achieve the behavior we desire. In fact, it's better to inspire your dog to want to follow your lead than it is to harshly control his behavior.

Think of your dog as a toddler that's never going to completely grow up. Over time, from puppyhood to adulthood, your dog learns to make better decisions. Over time, he is allowed more freedom. When he can prove that he makes wise decisions on his own, according to the rules of the household, he earns the right to have his space. However, he always knows that, when his "mom" or "dad" step in, he is to comply with their will over his own.

When I was young, my father used to say, 'This isn't a democracy.' When he told me to do something, I was expected to do it and not talk back. As a child, I was not old enough or mature enough to make all of my own decisions. Neither is your dog! Of course, he has a lot of decisions that are his own. In fact, it's nothing short of a miracle that these little creatures live in our house and choose to behave well. But when a parent tells a child that something needs to be done, only one party should prevail. It's the same with dogs.

Doesn't it make sense that in most situations, the adult with the most life experience and maturity should be making the rules?

How can a dog be expected to make the right decisions in a human world without human leadership?

It's all very logical, when you stop to think about it. Nature has designed life to work this way. If we can adapt our way of thinking to this plan, we are actually working with nature instead of against it.

When you tell a child to clean his room or do his homework, there are times that he doesn't want to. He will try to find a way around it. He'll whine, complain, pretend he doesn't hear you, walk away or hide. Children will try several tactics to get out of doing something they don't want to do. They try to negotiate, become defiant, and cry. They test our authority. If any of these methods works, the child will file that knowledge away in the back of his mind. Next time, he will remember what technique helped him get out of doing what he was told to and use it again.

However, if your child tries all of these techniques and none of them work, he will remember that, too!

Your dog is the same way. I always say that it's a dog's job to test your authority. It's part of his instinct to see if the pack leader qualifies for the job. If he refuses, avoids, snaps or runs away and you don't follow through to make your command happen, he learns that this behavior works. Each time afterward that you give that same command; the dog remembers that he got away with not complying. Therefore, he learns that there is no reason he has to obey you.

If he can dominate you in these small situations, why should he trust you to handle bigger threats as his leader?

If you say "sit" and your dog refuses and you give up after a couple of tries, then what kind of leadership does that display to a dog?

You appear to be the kind of leader that asks a few times, if he doesn't feel like it, then your dog doesn't really have to listen. That's not the kind of relationship either of you really wants.

Your dog's instinct is to test you.

He needs to know that he can't get one over on you. If he can, then nature tells him that he should be leader of this pack. If he can't get one over on you, then you are obviously more qualified to be the boss than he is. You have taken that control; therefore, you deserve to have it.

Now, just to be clear, frustration and anger never help us achieve leadership. If our dog is not complying, we are going to get far better results by being calm, quiet and authoritative. Once we use frustration, anger or loudness, we are losing. No dog wants to follow a leader that is not in control.

When you give your dog a command and he complies, you are being dominant.

When your will wins over his, you are the dominant one.

It doesn't have to involve shouting or frustration. You should never be mean to your dog. Dominance simply means that your will wins over the dog's will. When he complies, you are the more dominant one.

It is so important that we don't abuse this privilege of leadership. If your dog turns over his authority to you, it is your responsibility to be fair and loving with that position. If he is willing to surrender to the idea of you as his leader, boss and parent, it's your turn to show love and compassion in return. This is the beginning of a lifetime bond between you that is among the most beautiful relationships on earth. Treat it with respect and reverence.

Dominance can often be quite passive. I have trained many dogs that simply plop down and refuse to move. One dog I worked with, Roscoe, a coonhound mix, would gladly go on a walk with you. He was great on the leash, happy to follow and comply with the person walking him and quick to follow commands. However, when he was ready for the walk to be over, he would stop wherever he was, sit down and refuse to move. When I stopped and turned to see what was going on, Roscoe had just dominated me. He didn't really have to do anything. He simply dominated the walk by sitting down. I ended up lifting him into a standing position and leading him with my voice and the leash until he complied. I gave him no choice. If I allowed his behavior to work, he would know he could control the walk and me, as well.

There are no hard and fast rules about how to achieve leadership with your dog. This is a relationship. Just like any relationship, there are variables. However, as with any relationship, our behavior teaches others how to treat us. If we let people (or dogs) walk all over us, we are teaching them that we are pushovers. We are letting them know that they don't have to listen to us and they can basically do whatever they want to. If we are strong and commanding, others are more likely to respect us and comply with what we ask of them. If we temper this strength with affection and love, that's when we become more than just leaders. We become people to be looked up to and admired! We are worthy of respect. We're strong, confident, in control, yet loving, compassionate and kind. That is the ideal pack leader!

KEEP IT SIMPLE

It's amazing the way some people speak to their dogs. I've seen everything from yelling to baby talk to whispers to screams. I have yet to hear a dog communicate in any of these ways. If I heard a dog talk to me the way some owners talk to them, I would keel over in shock!

I always encourage people to watch their dogs, listen and observe. In general, there is not a lot of vocal activity going on. A dog will bark or growl or howl. However, I have never once heard a dog say, 'I told you to get off the couch!' or 'Stop peeing on my carpet!' or 'Hey, you're bothering me! Could you please move away from me? Thanks!' That's why it amazes me when people think their dog will understand these long, complicated sentences, conversations and yelling.

Don't get me wrong!

I am the first to have long, drawn out conversations with my dogs. I might even baby talk to them now and then or sing little songs. But I'll deny it if you ever tell anybody I admitted that!

I understand that they connect with the tone of our voice and the general emotion we are sending their way. In fact, I encourage people to talk to their dogs lovingly. When your dog is in a relaxed, peaceful or balanced state of mind, sweet sounding conversation translates to them as praise and affection.

When you share these traits at the right time, you are encouraging the behavior and state of mind they are in. They begin to tune in to the tone, sounds and intentions of our voice. I guarantee, though, our dogs are not getting the detailed meaning of most of these sentences. They are not absorbing the subtle nuances of our speeches. However, they do learn many of our words. They start to understand a lot of phrases we use that translate to them as love and affection. The feelings we intend to share become clearer the longer our dogs live with us. But I really don't think they are deciphering the human definitions of our "love speak". They have simply adapted to these pleasant sounds as a way we show love, warmth and affection.

They associate these words with what is going on at the time the word is being said. They have associative minds that say, "This equals that." Whereas humans reason. "If this happens, then that happens, then that and that." We form long chains of thought and the ability to put many different ideas together at a time. Dogs don't have the same kind of complex reasoning.

For these reasons, dogs have taught me so much about simplifying and living in the moment. We often have a tendency to think many steps down the line with a hundred "what ifs" and "whys" and "hows." Dogs just stay in the moment.

Have you ever noticed how people treat us when we are calm, simple, direct and to the point with our actions and words?

Look at how dogs handle things. I have learned from them how to make my everyday encounters so much simpler. When I'm calm, it calms those I'm talking to. When I'm quiet, people will bring their voices down. When I'm simple, others get to the point quickly and easily. Just by changing my behavior, I change each encounter around me, with animals and humans!

If we simply quiet our minds and voices and tune into what our dog is doing in the moment, it's amazing how much control we have. Alpha dogs exhibit this control all the time. By being still, relaxed and confident they achieve leadership so much faster than if they try to demand it. This is a simple lesson dogs taught me about life in general. The results around me are always better when I am calm, relaxed, quiet and in control of myself, first.

It's important that we understand this when we are correcting or telling our dog to do something. The shorter the phrase, the more to the point we make our statement, the easier it is for our dog to wrap their mind around the ideas we're conveying. When we are quiet and calm, we bring our dog's energy level down to ours, instead of trying to rise above theirs. It's so much easier to exert an influence by being of a different energy level than by trying to "out shout" our dog or use physical strength.

Our dogs hear four to five times the intensity level that we hear. They can pick out detailed sounds from long distances. They can identify amazingly subtle differences in tone and pitch. Imagine what yelling sounds like to them! Now, magnify the intensity of each sound they hear by five times and that is the way your dog is hearing it.

That's why shouting at your dog is so ineffective!

When we raise our voices, we are overwhelming our dog with sound and actually moving further away from the goal we are trying to achieve.

If you have a child and your child spills milk by mistake, what do you do?

You make a correction that fits the situation. You might simply say, 'Be a little more careful next time.' You don't scream or blow an air horn in your child's ears! Not only would that be ineffective, it would be terrifying, even cruel. The lesson would probably be all but forgotten and getting you to stop screaming would become the primary goal.

If your dog has an accident or does something you don't like, screaming has a similar effect. Panic, yelling, jerking their collar and dragging them around only harm your lesson. These actions actually lead your dog to shut down and not learn the point you are trying to make. However, if you correct in a swift, firm, but fair way, your dog connects the correction to the lesson. He realizes you just don't want him to do that particular behavior. You don't hate him. You just disagree with what he is doing at that moment.

Before I started teaching dogs, I studied them extensively. I watched their behaviors, their communication skills and their every day, moment-to-moment interaction. I wanted to know what motivated them, what made them tick, how they approached life. Long before I was able to articulate their language and know on a conscious level what they were saying, I simply watched, learned and tried to move around in their world.

It became clear to me that dogs do not have conversations that are anything like the conversations we have as humans. They communicate quite effectively, though. They "speak" very clearly and they get right to the point. So much was being said with a simple sound or a look or a nip. They let other dogs know in no uncertain terms exactly what they want without a single human word.

People often tend to over explain things. We worry about being polite and socially acceptable. We beat around the bush and embellish and include details in our stories that don't always need to be there. We over analyze, over think and sometimes say much more than is necessary. We want to paint a picture, give the person we are talking to an idea and an image to demonstrate what we are saying. We want to be entertaining and interesting. This is not even close to the way dogs do it.

A dog wants to get to the point. He doesn't have time to tell you a lot of the extraneous details or worry that he might be rude or hurting someone's feelings. A dog keeps things simple. If he wants you to stop something, he tells you "stop!" in his own way. If he wants you to move, he tells you to "move!" in his own way. He doesn't say please, he doesn't say thank you and he never says I'm sorry. He can't! He's not even capable of it!

Dogs are certainly not worried about keeping the conversation entertaining, either. I think we, as humans, try to keep our conversations interesting and we want to be at least somewhat engaging. Your dog just wants what he wants in the moment and he goes straight to the heart of getting it. He doesn't care if you're entertained.

The most amazing thing about all of this is, we love our dogs anyway! This is one of the most valuable lessons I have learned from dogs. They can jump on me, shove me out of the way, refuse to listen, defy me, ignore me, resist me and more! They have peed on my carpet, barked incessantly, chewed my belongings and jumped on my bed with their muddy feet. No matter how rude they might appear, how do I feel about them? I love them, anyway! How beautiful is that?

Isn't it nice to know that we don't have to do anything to be loved? It's the greatest lesson of all, if we can just learn to accept it. We can simply be who we are and our dogs will love us just for that! We don't have to make our dogs love us. In fact, we can't. They have to choose to, just like humans.

Dogs are too focused on making themselves happy, their leader happy or simply just surviving. They don't have time to waste on things like etiquette. This is a powerful lesson. It doesn't mean we have to be rude or stop having manners. In fact, I think it's very important to teach our dogs manners. They need to have rules and boundaries if they are going to live happily in our human society. They need to meet us in the middle and learn a few things about what behavior is expected of them. But these are people traits, taught to help them live more comfortably in a human world.

Everyone needs to know what behavior is expected of them. It makes life go smoothly. It helps us engage socially. Your dog will make many more friends and be welcome in many more places if he has learned manners from you. All I ask is that you teach him in a way he can grasp. Give him the opportunity to please you and get his mind around the lesson. Keep it simple.

The longer I live, the more I believe people appreciate it when I get to the point. It almost never helps a situation to add language and ideas that don't propel the conversation forward. When someone asks you to do something, there is nothing wrong with simply saying, "No".

"No, thank you," is nice, too. But when we veer off into a dialogue about all of the surrounding circumstances leading up to our "no" I think people would often just rather hear the simple answer. The life story is not necessary.

Often, we "over explain" to comfort ourselves. We are worried what people will think of us, will I hurt their feelings or will they dislike me? We go on and on until we feel more comfortable. We end up trying to reassure ourselves, when the person we are saying no to most likely doesn't care. What a waste of time and energy!

The point I'm trying to make is that Simplicity is the key. When you are talking to your dog, let's try to remember his brain operates in an entirely different way than ours does. He doesn't have long, reasoning thoughts. He doesn't decipher things in the same analytical, complex way that we do. He can't do math or drive a car. He can, however, understand you if you will reach out and meet him in the middle. Your dog would greatly appreciate it if you would keep things simple when asking him to do something or correcting him. He would be so thankful if you would learn a few simple things about his language and try to keep your expectations reasonable.

WE ALL HAVE NEEDS

I'm amazed when owners are baffled that their dogs don't automatically know everything that is expected of them.

Why does this dog go to the bathroom in the house?

Why does he go crazy when the doorbell rings?

Why won't he stop begging for food at the table?

My first question about any behavior is, "What have you done to teach the dog what is expected of him?"

Many times the answer is that they haven't done much. A lot of times, the owner is not very engaged with the dog until he does something wrong. Then, there is a lot of yelling and panic and frustration. That's sort of like hoping your child knows how to read without you teaching him how. Then, when he can't read, you hit him with a newspaper or scream in his ear.

It doesn't make much sense, does it?

For example, why should your dog know how to act at the door if you have never taken him to the door, on a leash, and demonstrated to him how to act with the doorbell rings? Until you do, that door represents a visitor, excitement, attention and, probably, the most exciting thing that has happened for the dog all day! Why should he act any other way but elated? Expecting anything different is like taking a child to the gates of Disney World and saying, "Now, don't be excited!"

Ridiculous, isn't it?

I once visited a couple with a toy poodle named Diamond. They kept the dog in a kennel all night. Then, when they woke up, they took the dog outside and tied her to a stake in the ground. While they got ready for work, the dog spent that time tied in a very small area outside. When they left for work, they returned the dog to her kennel. The dog stayed there for an eight-hour workday. When the couple returned home at night, they let the dog back out on the tie out.

The dog did come inside to spend a little bit of time with the couple. However, they wanted the dog to remain only in areas of their apartment that didn't have carpet. This meant the kitchen, the bathroom or the living room, but only when supervised. They became frustrated when the dog got excited. They wanted her to calm down and stop running around and jumping on them. Otherwise, back in the kennel.

The couple called me because they were fed up and frustrated with their dog's behavior. They couldn't understand why the dog was jumping, barking, frantic and crazy. Isn't that amazing? What seems so glaringly obvious to me as a dog lover was completely baffling to this couple. Could anyone be calm and perfectly behaved given the circumstances this dog was living under? I don't think so.

Dogs have simple needs. Every dog wants to know, "What is my position in this pack and what is expected of me?" Without this, your dog is a little bit lost. He craves structure. He desires routine. He wants boundaries.

A dog's first desire is to know his leader. Once we've established that with him, it helps him relax. If somebody doesn't step forward to take control, there is no order to life, in a dog's mind. However, we tend to love on our dog, baby talk to our dog and do all sorts of odd, weird behaviors but provide no restrictions.

To a dog, that must seem bizarre!

There's nothing wrong with any of that, in the right balance. In fact, dogs often grow to love that kind of treatment. They learn that this is how we express our love to them. Believe me, dogs are all about receiving love and affection!

When this kind of affection goes overboard, though, it can create an array of problems. Some dogs begin to perceive this as a kind of weakness. If there are no boundaries, no consequences for bad behavior, then why obey? Why listen to your rules?

It's important that we learn to balance our affection. Kids don't receive non-stop baby talk and praise twenty-four hours a day and neither should a dog! It has to be balanced with structure, rules, discipline and boundaries. There is nothing wrong with providing those things. They are all a part of loving your dog!

If we have a child and never make that child go to school, clean their room, carry their dishes to the sink or go to bed at a reasonable hour, what kind of child are we raising? Rules and structure *are* a form of love. I guarantee, your dog will be eternally grateful for kind but firm leadership.

Since you now know how important a strong leader is to your dog, you can feel better knowing that with a little bit of strength and structure, you are providing your dog with something he deeply desires. You are fulfilling his instinct and going with nature instead of against it.

You will find that as your relationship to your dog becomes more balanced, your bond will begin to deepen. Dogs adore their leaders and tend to feel enormous affection for the one that provides that leadership. They want to please their leader. If you take on that role and balance it with love and affection, you can only imagine how much your dog will love you for it!

UNSPOKEN MESSAGES

It has been said that only 7% of our communication is verbal. Another 38% depends on intonation or the sound of our voice. For example, a shaky voice may indicate that a person is shy, intimidated, or nervous. A loud, clear voice may indicate that a person is confident.The largest part of communication is body language, which makes up the remaining 55%. This tells me that a person who knows how to control their body and voice would be considered more appealing and more likely to be taken seriously.

Obviously, dogs don't speak English. They don't speak French, German or Chinese either! However, they do learn a lot of our words and how to properly respond when these words are spoken. There are many arguments about whether or not dogs truly understand the meaning of the words they are told. Do they really know what sit means or do they just associate it with what to do when we say it? Nobody knows for sure. Either way, I believe it is a miracle of nature that they even respond to our words at all.

Think about it.

In the wild, nobody says words to a dog. They don't have the capability of saying any words, themselves. But when they come to live with us, they want so badly to understand us that they begin to reach out. They work at learning and absorbing our ways of communicating. There is no reasonable explanation as to why this would work, but it does. It's a beautiful thing!

That's why I think it's so important that we take the time to reach back and learn some of our dog's language. They spend all day watching, listening, learning and observing us. They're like little sponges, absorbing everything about us! More than just learning what we want from them, they watch how we behave, what motivates us and I'm sure it all looks a little strange, from their point of view!

First and foremost, let's remember that our dog's brain does not receive information in the same way our human brain does. They don't filter the world's input at all the way we do. They don't have the ability to reason through a situation, observing it from all angles, project the outcomes or think about the consequences the way we can. Their brain simply doesn't work that way.

For the most part, a dog's brain reacts. They follow an instinctual, animal thought process that is simply reacting. They are not thinking about how their actions will affect their future. In fact, they don't project into the future at all. Your dog is almost always living completely and fully in the moment. Isn't that amazing? They don't worry about their careers or the mortgage or how things will be a week, a month or a year from now. They simply concern themselves with right now.

Humans could learn a lot from this way of thinking. When your dog is overjoyed to see you when you come home at the end of the day, he's not thinking about anything else but being fully engaged in celebrating your arrival. He's not embarrassed by his behavior. He is certainly not worried about getting your clothes dirty when he jumps on you. He's definitely not concerned about how hard your day at the office was or whether or not you want to play. He is simply reacting to your arrival home and letting the world know how happy he is to see you.

Of course, in this moment, if your dog does jump on you and get your clothes dirty, we often have a swift and emotional reaction in return. It must be baffling for your dog to see you get mad or frustrated when he is simply trying to tell you how much he loves you.

Imagine a four-year-old child running up, throwing their arms around you and saying, "I love you!" In response, you shove them and say, "Get away from me!" How bizarre would that be?

Of course, I'm not saying we shouldn't teach our dog manners. Of course, we should! I'm just asking why it's so hard for us to see this behavior for what it is and be patient and understanding. Your dog truly does not have the ability to think through how it's going to make you feel to be jumped on. He has no idea how much your outfit cost. He's just showing love the way all dogs show love to each other. Other dogs would accept this behavior and think it was fantastic!

In our world, however, most people aren't too fond of dirty dog paws all over their clothes. Your dog needs to know how you, his leader, feel about this kind of behavior. As a consequence of your reaction, he will learn to control his excitement over seeing you and behave in a new way. His actions won't change because he reasoned, "Gee, my Dad got his pants dirty from my paws on him. Now he'll have to have them cleaned and pressed all over again." His actions will change because he has learned, as a follower of the alpha of the pack, that his leader does not like this behavior. His leader wants a very different kind of approach.

If we can learn in these moments to observe our own reactions even more closely than our dog's actions, we will achieve much faster results. If our dog is not complying, then, nine times out of ten, it is because we are not communicating our desires in a language he can understand. The more words we throw at the dog, the louder we yell and the more emotional we get, the further we are away from getting the behavior we want.

Emotional reactions are very uncomfortable for a dog. Our emotional outbursts confuse the situation and confuse our dog. Our anger, frustration and disappointment are complex. The message is clouded by how you feel in that moment. As hard as it may seem, if you can separate yourself from the emotion in your correction and stick with a swift, split second burst of sound, the outcome is likely to be exactly what you want it to be. Just remove the feelings about it.

We need to keep our corrections simple enough that our dog can get his brain around them. "I told you to stop jumping on me!" Do you really think he knows what that means? I can assure you, your dog never took an English class, never dissected a sentence and never, ever went to high school. Therefore, I think it's safe to say, he doesn't have the reference tools to be on the same page with what you're saying. By talking on and on, you are setting your expectations way to high.

How do dogs make corrections?

Well, first of all, they use a much more simple form of communication. They stick to the basics and try to convey, with minimal language, what it is they desire. They don't beat around the bush. They don't enhance or embellish. They simply get to the point and move on.

Once we understand these simple facts about our dog, communication becomes easy. Once we learn just a few basics about dog language, we are off and running! Most dogs already have an innate desire to please their leader. Once you simplify your language to a level they can understand, your bond to your dog strengthens and your relationship becomes that much deeper and more connected.

I have found that clients of mine who have the most trouble getting their dogs to comply are the people who are least aware of their own behavior. A lot of people simply don't know how they appear. They don't know what image they are projecting, how they are using their voice and they can't see themselves the way the world sees them.

When I work with people who are very self-aware and in charge of who they are, they tend to have much more success with their dogs. That's because they tune in to how they are using their voices, what kind of presence are they showing and what they are specifically doing in each interaction with their dog. It's so much more about us learning how to connect than it is about teaching our dog anything!

I worked with a woman once who had a very fearful dog named Becca, who was a medium sized rescue dog, shaggy, very cute and very insecure. She would bark, lunge and then retreat backwards, sending the very clear message, "Stay away from me! You make me nervous!" Most of her behavior was a big bluff, but a time or two; she actually tried to bite people.

When I arrived, Becca's owner was holding her on a leash, standing several feet behind the dog, while Becca barked and lunged and tried to get away. There was a lot of shouting and pulling, frustration and fear. After a little time passed and I took control of Becca's leash, we all sat down and began to talk.

Becca's owner began to tell me she was a very nervous person, unsure, eager to please everyone and didn't feel in control in most areas of her life. She had trouble being a "boss" in all areas and this included dealing with her dog. She simply wanted a loving lap dog with no issues. However, that's not what she adopted.

I believe that many times God doesn't give us the dog we desire, he gives us the dog we need. As in other areas of our life, we don't always know what's best for ourselves. Wrapped up in these little creatures are endless lessons about life and ourselves. All we have to do is look for them.

Have you ever had what appeared to be a bad situation, only to look back and see the powerful lesson you learned from those circumstances? We grow from challenges. Sometimes we are presented with just the right situation to force us to look at ourselves and grow to be better people. I believe dogs give us this gift over and over if we will just pay attention.

Becca's mom gradually began to open up to the idea that her nervousness was, in turn, making Becca nervous. This little dog had had a very sad background. She had to fend for herself for a long time before she came to live in her forever home. As a puppy, she didn't have proper guidance or training. She simply developed a way to survive, without a pack to depend on. Now that she was living in a safe, secure home full of love, she didn't know how to let her guard down. How should she know who is safe to trust and who is not?

At this point in a dog's development, they don't need someone to come down to their level and feel sorry for them. They don't want a partner in their out of control feelings. They want a strong leader to pull them out of their situation and lead them to safety. They want someone in control to rescue them. If you were drowning, you wouldn't want someone to jump in the water with you and tell you how everything is going to be alright. You would want someone strong to pull you to safety and show you a solution that would save you.

Becca wasn't about to turn her fears and anxieties over to someone unsure, scared, nervous or weak. By being nervous, the only example Becca was being given was a bad one. Every time a stranger entered the room, Becca's mom became nervous. The dog had no way of knowing her mom was becoming nervous because of her behavior. As far as Becca could see, here comes a stranger and that's what's making my mom nervous. No one is taking care of the situation, so I guess it's up to me. It looks like I'm the strongest one here. Thus, the barking and lunging.

Once her owner learned to become strong, project a demeanor of control and act sure of herself, Becca began to relax and turn over her authority. Gradually, in every new situation they encountered, when Becca lost control, her owner took over. Becca began to believe that her mom would not lead her into a dangerous situation. If a situation did become dangerous, it was now clear that her mom knew what to do and was sure enough and strong enough to handle it. Her behavior began to change for the better very quickly. She is now the gentle, sweet, love of her family's life!

It's really not that hard to understand how your dog sees you. In fact, if you open your eyes, your mind and your heart, most of the answers are right there.

THROUGH YOUR DOG'S EYES

Aside from changing and observing our own behaviors, how can we learn to speak this magic "dog language"?

Before I get into specifics, I'd like to point something out. When we raise children, we don't wait until something goes wrong to teach them. In fact, we are teaching them, both subconsciously and consciously, from the day they are born. Through our voices, our actions, our expressions, our expectations and so much more, our children learn all day, every day from us. They are like little sponges, absorbing and observing, even when we are oblivious to this fact. Sometimes we are teaching actively, sometimes passively. In either case, our children take in and digest every little thing we do and say.

Over time, our children begin to learn how to treat us. They learn who we are in relation to them. They learn whether or not to respect us, to listen to us and to obey. Are we people that should be heard, honored and respected? Maybe we are pushovers and let them get their way all of the time. We all have our own, unique style of parenting. No matter what kind of parent we are, though, it seems like it is every child's job to at least try to get around our rules. Its one way nature has designed us to see whether or not we can trust our leader.

Is my leader stronger than me?

Is he better equipped to lead than I am?

Is this a person worthy of turning my authority over to or is this someone I can easily get one over on?

Whether or not we enforce our rules and set firm boundaries helps determine whether or not we are worth listening to.

As children, we have to learn the limits. Sometimes, the only way to figure this out is to try to get around the rules. Then, Mom or Dad step in and let us know we have crossed the line.

Over time, our children learn whether or not they should take us seriously. We demonstrate over time what kind of person we are and our children respond accordingly. Then, when a big issue comes along, they either listen or they don't based on how they view us.

In exactly the same way, our dogs decide how to treat us based on our behaviors toward them all day long. We are constantly being given opportunities to teach. If we emerge the leader in these small moments, it is so much more likely our dog will listen to us in a crucial moment later on.

When we tell our children to clean their room, do their homework or go to school we are, in a sense, loving them. It wouldn't be a very well rounded relationship if we just poured on affection and food all day long and never made a correction. If we never had a rule or an expectation, what kind of child would we be raising? We do each of these things so that when our child is a young adult, they will make good decisions on their own. We balance our love and affection with rules and authority so that our children learn to be responsible grown ups. We also do these things so our children know how to treat us.

Our every day actions in the presence of our dog add up to how they are going to view us and treat us. If we are passive, disengaged and don't have an ongoing, all day relationship with our dog, why should he listen to us? A lot of people get busy with their own lives, work and interests and tend to forget how little attention the dog is getting. He doesn't ask for much. You can include him in your every day life so easily!

We have so many things that occupy our minds. We go to work, school, play sports, go shopping, go to dinner, see movies, go out with friends, read, watch T.V. Our dog sits at home and waits for something to happen. Most times, you are the source of that "something" happening. If you don't engage and throw the ball, bring him to the park, walk him or simply spend time with him, what is he supposed to do?

Your dog has a very intelligent mind. He has needs just like we have needs. The beauty of having a dog is that it doesn't take that much to make him happy. Exercise, play, food, a warm place to sleep, a couple of toys, his leader's approval… that's about it.

Many times, our needs and schedules run in opposition to our dog's. We get up in the morning after a full night of sleep. Our dog is fully charged and ready to go! Unfortunately, we have to go to work. We put our dog outside for a little bit. He relieves himself and then comes back inside. Worse, sometimes we walk the dog out on a leash, tell him to, "Hurry up!" and then run back inside. We shower and dress and head off to work. Your dog then sits all day, alone and without mental stimulation, waiting for you to return. Work ends, we return home and there is our dog, having napped and re-energized all over again. He's ready to rock! We, on the other hand, are dead on our feet, exhausted from the day's work. "Get off me! Stop jumping! What's the matter with you?" Then, we eat, feed our dog, he gets some play time (hopefully!) then it's off to bed. What has his day been like? Not too thrilling, huh?

Our dog is a living, breathing, thinking, feeling being with needs and desires. He has a life, too! When we adopt him, we are accepting and committing to the responsibility of honoring these needs and desires. We can't just take in a dog and expect him not to behave like a dog. It is not realistic.

I believe dog adoption is a serious, lifelong commitment. Just like adopting a child, you should not take on the responsibility of caring for another life unless you are prepared to stick with it. Only under the most extreme, dire, helpless circumstances should you ever give up on caring for your dog yourself. Even if you must re-home him, it is your responsibility to make sure he is well cared for, wherever he goes. He is a member of your family.

When we begin to look at life from our dog's point of view, we begin to open our hearts to so many ways we can deepen our relationships. When we provide for our dogs needs and desires, not only does the dog blossom, but you will find yourself changing, as well. One of the most beautiful things about the human/dog bond is that a living creature outside of ourselves depends so completely on us. Doesn't it make you feel special to know another being has turned over his whole life, well-being, health and safety to you? I always say, my dog makes me feel very important. He needs me!

Now, imagine what a betrayal it is to take on this responsibility and then neglect or abuse him. It's inexcusable. It really takes so little to make your dog happy. I encourage you to make the effort.

Let's start with our voices. Even though our dogs don't understand the details of our whole sentences and paragraphs, they do connect to our tone of voice. Simply talking to your dog in a loving tone is an easy place to start. By lovingly connecting to your dog with your soft, sweet tone of voice, he begins to feel good about you. He learns that this is a human way of sharing affection.

The best thing about conversation with our dog is that we can do it any time, anywhere. We don't have to stop getting ready for work or making dinner. We can simply add a little conversation and connect with our dogs. Saying their name, talking to them about everything and nothing at all can help connect you to him. Obviously, he doesn't know exactly what you're telling him. He doesn't care about traffic on the freeway or your big promotion at work. What he is connecting to is the emotion you are expressing. He is bonding with the intent behind your voice.

For people who find it hard to find the extra time to share with their dogs, adding conversation to your daily routine is a great place to start. I speak to my dogs every time I pass them in the house. It takes little or no effort to say hello in the hallway or give them a scratch or pat them on my way to doing something else. Each word we exchange is a little mental stimulation, a little connection, and a little boost of self-esteem. And it does wonders for the way I feel, as well. A little conversation goes a long way!

Exercise is so important, too. It is the key for some dogs to be able to think straight. Imagine if you had no physical stimulation. Imagine sitting still all day, every day with no outlet. That's nearly impossible for most people and it is certainly inconceivable for most dogs! They are built to run and roam and explore! When your dog is confined all day with no outlet, it begins to affect his ability to think clearly. He can't concentrate on anything except, "How do I get all of this energy out?"

One of your dog's fundamental, crucial needs is exercise. Granted, some dogs need more exercise than others. That is why you should get to know your particular dog as well as you can before adopting. Does this dog fit my lifestyle? Is this dog a good fit for my energy level? Will I be able to fulfill this dog's needs?

There are so many creative ways to exercise your dog. Some dogs get tired after a little ball throwing. Other dogs need miles of running and still can't slow down. Other dogs need tasks and jobs to occupy their mental activity. It's our job to assess what activities best suit our dog and help them to fulfill those basic needs.

A Border Collie, bred to work and think all day long herding cattle is a poor choice if you live in a high-rise apartment. It's also a terrible choice if you don't like to get outdoors and exercise every day. A Bassett Hound is not a good choice if you're a jogger who likes to run for miles and wants a companion for your running adventures.

A German Shepherd doesn't make a very good lap dog to sit around all day watching T.V.

I suggest doing a lot of research on breeds and their dispositions before you decide to commit to adopting a dog. I believe a dog adoption is a very serious commitment and you shouldn't go into it guessing or following impulsive decisions based on cuteness or "love at first sight".

BEAUTIFUL DIFFERENCES

If dogs don't communicate with words or reason through complicated chains of thought, if they don't listen to our long explanations of our frustrations and feelings, then how do they communicate?

The good news is, it's infinitely simpler than the language we humans use. Dogs don't have nouns and verbs and adjectives. They don't say one thing and mean another. They don't try to cover up their feelings or hide their intentions. They don't smile when they're sad or growl when they're happy. What you see is what you get. The feelings and intentions your dog displays are directly connected to what's going on inside of him.

Dogs are motivated by instinct. They react much more than they act. In other words, they are usually in a state of responding to outside stimulus. Much of the behavior we try to control is simply a reaction to something outside of them triggering that particular behavior.

They see a squirrel, they react.

They feel threatened, they react.

They smell food, they react.

While human beings are constantly thinking and creating and playing out scenarios in our heads, dogs are usually quite content to live in the moment and react to what's happening around them. They are not burdened by worry and "what ifs". They're not thinking about what might happen tomorrow, what happened yesterday or what life will be like years from now or even hours from now. They are simply living in the "now".

This is great news for us!

We don't have to feel sorry for what has happened to them in the past, fear what might happen in the future or dwell on all of the mistakes they have made or we might have made with them. We can simply address what's happening now and create the moment we want to create. Because we have the ability to reason, we can use this to our advantage. We can use our dog's nature to move him in the direction of desirable behavior and a happy relationship with us.

The first step is to work with nature and not against it. We're not trying to force behavior on your dog or make the dog do something that is against his nature. Our goal is to use the dog's natural instincts and desire to please us and themselves. We want our dog to want to make us happy. That is the ideal leader/dog relationship.

First, we must realize that dogs look at life as a hierarchy. Just like the military, they see other dogs as dominant, submissive, equal.

Are we above each other in the social order or below each other?

Does my person have a higher rank than mine or am I able to manipulate the outcome in my favor?

Just like a child who tests the rules and limits, a dog will try you with their behavior. Will you give in and give your dog his way or will you be a firm but fair leader who sets the rules in the house?

Just like a child who respects his parents is likely to try and make them proud of him, your dog will begin to exhibit behaviors he believes will make you happy. In return, it's our job to pour out the positive results and praise. Your dog should feel the "jackpot" of praise when he does the right thing. He will be motivated to seek out that warm, fuzzy feeling he gets from you. The more his behavior is associated with that feeling, the more he will exhibit that behavior.

By the same reasoning, if your corrections are short, appropriate and to the point, your dog will associate his negative behaviors with that result. Give him something he can work with, a message he can get his mind around, and he is likely to become the perfect pup in no time! Long sentences and yelling to correct a behavior are terrible ways to try to motivate your dog. The louder and longer the correction, the further away you are from achieving what you want.

Let's talk a little bit about those behaviors we don't want. What is an appropriate correction? Wouldn't it help to know a language that gets right to the point and allows your dog to understand exactly what you want? Lucky for us, it's not that complicated.

When your dog was first born, his mother began teaching him the fundamentals of dog communication. If the circumstances of your dog's early life allowed for it, he spent the first eight weeks after his birth with his mother and littermates. This was one of the most crucial times in the development of your dog. Mother dogs teach their puppies an amazing array of lessons in a few short weeks. They set the foundation for how your dog goes through life. Just like a human child, Mom helps them become well-rounded citizens equipped for facing life. It's the small, every day lessons that add up to a curriculum that prepares your dog for his adoption into your family.

Among the many, amazing behaviors a dog learns before he is eight weeks old is HOW to learn. The way in which your pup's mother corrects and praises, loves and withholds, leads and stands back all add up to a dog that is well equipped to receive your teaching. If we will learn just a few of Mom's methods and apply them, you will be amazed at how prepared your dog is to respond and accept your guidelines.

Within the first few seconds of your puppy's life, his mother does something that becomes synonymous with affection for the rest of his life. She licks him. It may turn your stomach a bit, but a mother dog will help her puppy remove his embryonic sack by biting, licking and yes, even eating it. As she licks the gooey stuff off of her new offspring, he is beginning to receive his first feelings of affection. For the rest of his life, this kind of licking becomes the very definition for him of warm, fuzzy feelings of love.

Most humans I know don't want to lick their dogs. As much as I love them, myself, I do not want to lick my dogs. However, every time we pet and stroke our dogs with our hands, we are evoking that early feeling of being licked. As we bond more deeply with our dog, he begins to seek out this affection. He begins to realize that when he performs certain behaviors he receives more of this affection and petting. Therefore, he begins to do more and more of these desired behaviors more often.

The early affection from his mother and littermates translates to an adult dog more accepting of touches. These touches and pets become his "language of love". In other words, we are actually mimicking something nature has provided to demonstrate to our dog that he is doing the right thing. He knows he is loved through a form of communication his mother instilled in him long before he met us. His mother has given us a shortcut we can use to demonstrate our feelings and praise him for being so wonderful.

Nursing comes next. Puppies are born with their eyes closed and it can take as long as a couple of weeks for them to open. Therefore, Mom's licks and cuddles and affection are a crucial part of their early development. Nursing is an enormous part of this early bonding experience.

Immediately after birth, your pup's mother provides affection, food, warmth and safety. That's a pretty good place to start! This is lesson number one that we learn from Mom. Providing these simple things strikes a chord deep inside your dog. He is associating your petting, affection, feeding and more with the love he received from day one.

Very soon after this initial phase, Mom Dog begins to balance her affection with discipline and structure. In most cases, there is a whole litter of puppies to organize. They don't have a sophisticated, complicated language to provide order to this very young pack. They don't have time for being cordial or beating around the bush. They need to get to the point so everyone immediately understands what is expected of them. It's up to the mother dog to keep her puppies safe and learn how to venture into life. This brings me to the "magic language" of correction.

THE MAGIC LANGUAGE

The secret is, there really is no "magic" to the language of dogs. In fact, from one dog to another, it's all pretty easy to understand. People, on the other hand, often look on baffled at what is happening in their dog's world. They don't read the signs and signals that are all so clear to other dogs. They are telling us stuff all the time. We just have to learn what to look and listen for.

I think that many of us have gotten so far away from the animal part of our instinct, it becomes challenging to just simplify our behavior. Animals, in general, use simple messages in a simple language and they get right to the point. We, the humans, step in and project our complicated ideas and theories onto the situation.

I have worked with all sorts of people with all sorts of ideas about what their dogs are thinking. People tell me their dog is mad, jealous, sad, afraid, happy and a thousand other things that often have no basis in the truth. Many times people are simply creating a story that goes with what they perceive the dog to be going through. In fact, most times, the owner is projecting their own issues onto the dog.

They are making the dog's behavior fit into a complex scenario that fits with that person's viewpoint of their own life.

I once worked with a woman and her Jack Russell Terrier mix. The dog was very aggressive around food and toys. He became particularly vicious when you turned your back. As you walked away, the dog would lunge at your feet and bite your shoes like crazy. The woman told me he was "sad" that the person was leaving. He was "mourning" the loss of that person and lashing out to express how upset he was at being left alone. She told me the dog had previously been neglected and dumped at a shelter. She believed that people leaving triggered the dog's feelings of abandonment and that he was trying to make them stay with him. I think she couldn't have been further from the truth.

In the language that dogs use with each other, they are very clear about the message they are sending to other dogs. They don't beat around the bush. They get right to the point.

Where did they learn how to do this?

From their mother, in the first few days of their life. She taught them exactly how to make a firm but fair correction and get the desired result immediately.

You've probably seen your dog wrestling and playing with another dog, having a good time. All of a sudden, one dog does something that the other dog doesn't like. His playmate plays too rough or bites too hard. He immediately gives a low, sharp, intense split second bark. The action freezes and both dogs stop in their tracks. This is how one dog tells another, "Stop it!"

His mother teaches this very basic action to a puppy from his earliest days of life. When he nurses too hard, plays too rough or does something dangerous, Mom steps in. She gives a brief, lightning fast correction. From the outside, it looks pretty harsh. To a person who has never seen this kind of correction, it can look like the mother dog might hurt her pup. But just as soon as the correction has begun, it is over.

This is one of the most valuable lessons we can learn from dogs. They don't hold a grudge. Once a correction is made and the puppy complies, the moment is over. We're back to being best friends. Dogs don't carry over the emotion of frustration or anger. They don't continue to punish a dog with prolonged lessons and hard feelings. Once the pup complies, the lesson is over.

If every person could learn just one lesson from this book, this might be the most life changing. Once a situation is corrected, there is no need to continue having bad feelings about it. What are we accomplishing by giving dirty looks, letting our dog (or anyone!) know how angry or upset we are. Once the moment has passed, the behavior is fixed and things are smooth, it does no good to keep holding on to the moment that has long past. Correct and move on.

Human beings often have a tendency to linger in their negative emotions. It's amazing how people will worry about what other people think of them, what was said or done a long time ago or what might happen in the distant future. We hang on to guilt, sadness and a lot of other feelings that serve no purpose. Dogs let go of the past and move on so much more easily than humans. This is one of the greatest lessons we can learn from them!

The ways in which our corrections are made are very important. I believe in using the least amount of correction needed to achieve the result we desire. If a simple, quiet "No!" is enough, why should we yell or scream? Some dogs are more sensitive than others, so a little sound goes a long way. If a dog is hypersensitive, then over correcting can actually damage the lesson or make the dog overreact in the future.

Dogs can hear at a level four to five times more intensely than we hear. Sounds that seem loud to us must be overwhelming to a dog. That's why yelling and screaming actually harms your lesson. When your dog is overwhelmed by sound, he can't think straight. He is more likely to forget the lesson you are trying to teach, entirely. When your dog is being yelled at, he is probably more concerned with making the sound stop than he is trying to figure out what you want from him.

If you have a child and your child spills milk, you don't hit him in the head with a baseball bat. You simply say, "Hey! Let's be more careful next time." We clean up the spill and learn the lesson that the moment has to offer us. I would encourage you to look at mistakes your dog makes in this same way. I believe accidents and mistakes are actually opportunities in disguise.

When your dog urinates in the house, I look at this as a chance to teach the dog, in his own language, that we don't do that in the house. We do that outside. How will he know what not to do unless he does it and is told not to? We've already discussed how a dog doesn't reason the same we do. How could he be expected to figure out what kind of bathroom habits we don't want unless he does them and we show him that it is not wanted?

Often, people are baffled that their dogs don't behave in a "prepackaged" human way. They don't come housebroken and knowing how to act in our home. Yet we talk to them like humans. We baby talk to them, scold them excessively, yell, get frustrated, ignore them, spoil them and a thousand other things that must seem crazy to a dog! We speak English to a creature that doesn't speak English, expecting them to instantly learn human behavior. Then, we go overboard and punish them for not knowing what we want. Isn't that insane?

When we have a dog in our house, that dog is constantly trying to figure us out. He is watching, learning, listening and trying to understand us. He reaches out to learn our ways, adapts, adjusts and tries to fit in. I think we owe it to him to reach back, even if it's only a little bit. It's only fair. Life is so much easier when we understand this "dog language" more clearly.

Our dog doesn't have huge expectations of us. Learning how to effectively communicate with him provides both you and him with so much! Look how happy your dog is with just a bowl of food, a dish of fresh water, a soft, warm bed, a toy and your attention. Wouldn't life be so wonderful if we could learn this from our dog! All of the things we think we need to be happy must seem like an endless list of meaningless stuff to our dog.

If your dog's needs are so simple, then maybe his thought process and communication skills are simple, too. We have to simplify our messages until they are in a form our dog can get his mind around. If our words and actions exceed what he can comprehend, then the message will certainly get lost in the mumbo jumbo.

WHAT HE'S *NOT* SAYING

If dogs don't use words, don't have complex reasoning and they don't over think things, we must learn how they do look at the world.

We talked earlier about how dogs are almost always reacting instead of acting. They are reacting to what is going on around them. Therefore, in a moment that calls for a correction, your dog is most likely reacting to a split second infraction. Most of the time, we miss this crucial moment. One dog has given another a dirty look or a threatening body posture or even a bite.

In a flash, your dog reacts. He doesn't think about consequences. He doesn't worry about politeness or hurting the other dog's feelings. He doesn't even think it through at all. He reacts. He gives that short, sharp, low bark. Maybe he gives a few short ones, right in a row. He moves forward, toward the other dog. By his tone, sharpness and body language, the other dog knows exactly what he means. If that dog complies and backs down, most of the time, that is the end of it. Your dog has just used one element of the universal language of dogs to stop unwanted behavior.

How can we recreate this moment for ourselves?

First, we need to learn to become more reactive. We're taught all of our lives to think before we speak, explore our options before we act and talk through a problem with people we are having a conflict with. Your dog doesn't understand this at all!

Imagine your dog is doing something you don't like. Whether it's urinating on the rug, chewing your shoe, jumping up on the furniture or burning down your house, the correction should always be the same.

You make your tone of voice low, short, sharp and percussive. "No!" or "Hey!" work great. You can say "Ah!" or "Quit!" I don't care if you say "Lamp!" or "Car!" As long as the sound tells him you mean it, the word you use is secondary. The sound and tone of your voice are the most important things.

When your dog makes a corrective bark to another dog, there is no word attached to the sound. There is only the bark. Your dog's brain is designed to receive this kind of sound as a message to stop his behavior. When you add a word to the sound, your dog begins to associate that word with the sound. Soon, we're making the sound less and using the word more. He learns this word and begins to associate it as the thing that means, "Stop it!"

This is somewhat of a miracle of nature. The fact that our dog learns our words at all is amazing! He does not have a spoken language in his world. There is nothing in his DNA that can explain why he would be able to learn our words, but he does! He doesn't even have the part of the brain that can create verbal language. However, they love us so much that they reach out and attempt to understand our language. Isn't that beautiful?

Before you know it, your dog is learning to sit, stay, come, lie down and so much more. Theories vary on how many words a dog can learn. Most people believe that they can learn as many as 150 words. They do this out of necessity. They live in our world and in order to get along and understand what's going on, they watch, listen, study and absorb. We should at least have the courtesy of learning a few things about their world, in return.

From the moment you first use this low, sharp bark, your dog will get it. He knows what that means.

I have seen dogs I've worked with light up the first time they hear me make this sound. They seem so grateful to hear someone speak to them in their own "native tongue" that they are immediately drawn to me, eager to please. Granted, this doesn't happen every time with every dog. But I can tell you it has happened to me many times.

Just because the sound is associated with a correction, a dog will not resent you for it. They simply react to the sound. When properly used, this correction sound can actually bond your dog more closely to you. It's a fair correction as opposed to yelling. You're now speaking his language. You're giving him the gift of being able to understand your intentions without muddying up the message! This is very comforting to a dog.

Dogs bark for many different reasons. Not all barks are alike. Some are for warning; some show excitement and other barks express fear. However, the one time, short, sharp, low bark shows that you are in control. It shows strength and most often means "Stop!" I also use a slightly softer variation for commands. Using your voice in this way shows the dog you are serious, strong, you mean business and you expect immediate compliance.

Once your dog complies with what you want, it is time to immediately shift gears. You must not follow your correction with extra "stuff". Don't cloud the lesson by prolonging the correction.

Many times, a dog will immediately go back to playing with a dog that has just corrected them. They don't hold a grudge. A mother dog will immediately return to loving her pup the second her correction is finished. Dogs don't grumble and complain and go on and on with commentary about the incident. "I can't believe you peed on my rug! That's a $500 rug! Why can't you learn to go outside?"

The worst, to me, is when people call their dog names or curse. Of course, dogs don't know the specific meaning of these insults or put-downs. However, those tones of voice, backed up by harsh emotion and frustration definitely have a negative impact on your dog. If someone yelled at you, made nasty faces and frustrated body movements, whether you understood the words or not, you would clearly get the message. Your dog does, too.

When we send these negative messages, we are damaging the trust our dog has for us. Fortunately, our dogs are very forgiving. Their love is unconditional and they give us so many opportunities at forgiveness. Isn't that a beautiful lesson? How many stories have we all heard about dogs with an abusive, neglectful background that come back with love and affection for human beings? Could you do the same for a dog?

I know a lot of people who have had bad experiences with dogs. They have been bitten or mauled. They approach every dog from that point forward with fear and apprehension. Wouldn't it be an incredible thing if we took a lesson from our dogs? If we could forgive the dogs (or people!) in our past and move on, wouldn't life be so much easier?

At the very least, I think it is wonderful when we can approach each new dog with a clean slate. As much as dogs have in common, they are all different with different personalities (or "dog-analities"). To say all dogs are scary or mean or dumb or defiant is like saying all people have those qualities. It is absolutely untrue.

Dogs have bitten me many times. I have almost had my finger bitten off. I have been clawed, shoved, scarred and tackled. However, each time, I get right back in the game and start with a fresh attitude. Most times I have found that the dog respects this and instantly changes his behavior toward me. Giving up is a weakness and dogs don't respect weakness.

I also approach each new dog with no preconceptions. Each dog I meet is a new individual with his own issues, attitudes, background and style. I can't impose my past judgments on him. That would be incredibly unfair! Would you like for people to judge you based on a jerk they met in the past? No, you probably wouldn't!

Our relationship with our dog begins with us. When we are calm or excited or fearful or aggressive, most of the time your dog will reflect this. If you are his leader and you exhibit unstable behavior, he is likely to exhibit unstable behavior, as well. Kids learn from their parents and dogs learn from their leaders.

Dogs are very intuitive. They know when you are upset or frustrated or calm or nervous or relaxed or fearful. Dogs have been trained to find cancer in human beings. They have been taught to help seizure patients, lead the blind and even alert diabetics when their insulin drops to a dangerous level. If they can do all of these things, they can certainly tell when your mood shifts. They know when you are afraid of them. They know when you are upset with them or happy about something. And they certainly know when you are unsure.

If you are alert enough and begin to connect to these abilities in your dog, you will begin to become more self-aware. You can start to monitor your own behavior by the way your dog is reacting to you. I often tell my clients that when your dog is not complying with your commands, you should first check yourself.

Are you frustrated?

Are you raising your voice?

Are you upset or distracted by something else?

Are you sending out a barrage of words when you don't get what you want?

Dogs will do one of four things in the face of a threat or an unstable animal.

They will…

1. fight,
2. flee,
3. avoid
4. surrender.

They really don't make any other choices in the face of something they fear or don't quite understand. Imagine if you were apprehensive about someone approaching you. Let's pretend a person is walking toward you wearing a ski mask and holding a tire iron. This doesn't necessarily mean they are intending to harm you. However, in your experience, these signals mean danger.

In the face of danger, different people will behave in different ways.

Would you run?

Would you smile as you passed and pretend nothing was wrong?

Would you turn another way?

Maybe you would jump on them and subdue them first before they could get you?

Remember, your dog has a very strong survival instinct. He is an animal, much more in touch with his prehistoric, animal roots. When he is unclear about another creature's intentions, he is most likely to err on the side of survival. When we act in a way that is interpreted as threatening to our dog, he's going to react in one of the only four ways he knows, either fight, flee, avoid you or surrender to you.

The decision your dog makes in the face of a perceived threat is determined by many factors.

What has his past been like?

Has he encountered situations like this before?

Has he been raised to trust humans or fear them?

Has he had a life of fear and abuse or one of love and patience?

What is his natural demeanor and personality?

All of us, human or animal, are informed by many different experiences, viewpoints and the life we have led. No two people are exactly alike, just like no two dogs are exactly alike.

We all frame our view of the world based on the life we have lived. Is the world your dog views a safe one? Are people his friends that bring love and affection? Maybe your dog views the world as a place to fear where people are known to be abusive and scary. Maybe he feels confident and in control. He makes up his mind based on what he has experienced.

I prefer that my dog obeys me not because he is afraid or intimidated by me. I prefer my dog listens because he respects me, trusts me and perceives me to be his leader. If he thinks I'm stable, not threatening, strong, decisive, trustworthy, to the point and that I mean what I say, he is very likely to surrender to my desires.

Isn't this the whole goal?

He surrenders to my will, but he is happy to! He loves me and our relationship is stronger and deeper because of our simple, direct communication and mutual respect. Because he has followed the rules and respected the boundaries of his leader and household, he receives a jackpot of love and affection!

Isn't that simple?

I think the ideal person/dog relationship has about 1% correction time and 99% love and affection.

If we are correcting our dogs, it should be over in a split second. Our correction should be directly associated with the unwanted behavior *while* that behavior is in action. The second your dog chooses to stop that behavior, then we should stop our correction immediately. He lets go of his behavior, therefore, we should let go of our correction.

In fact, you can praise his decision to stop. I believe the immediate contrast between the right and wrong makes the moment easier for the dog to identify. He feels the negative result during his bad behavior. The second it stops, he immediately feels the positive result.

Timing is everything in making a correction. Your dog has an associative mind. This means he associates what he is doing with what is going on around him. For example, if every time he has an accident in the house he gets hit, he will begin to associate that behavior with being hit. He is also associating going to the bathroom with whoever is hitting him. This begins to grow into a distrust of that person and even worse, the possibility of distrusting people altogether.

Hitting is never good. It is abusive and an over the top reaction to an offense that probably didn't warrant it in the first place. We don't hit a child when they make a mistake. Therefore, you should definitely not hit your dog, who is also a member of the family. Besides, dogs don't know what hitting is. They don't have hitting in their world. Dogs don't hit each other. It's not a part of their language. They don't even have hands!

When we correct a child for unwanted behavior, we try to make the punishment fit the crime. If he spills something or has an accident we try to make the level of our reaction match the level of the infraction. If we yell too loud, scream, stomp or even hit, not only have we lost the lesson but we've also damaged the trust of that child toward us. The result is not just a correction of the behavior or mistake, but we have hurt the emotions and self worth of the child. He is less concerned with the incident and more concerned with making the yelling, the hitting and the disapproval stop. He starts to worry about a much bigger picture than just the mistake he has made.

I don't think any of us wants this kind of result, with a child or with our dog. I can't count how many people I have worked with that have had over the top reactions to their dog's behavior. The dog soils the carpet or chews the furniture and the owner goes ballistic! The dog forgets the mistake entirely and begins to run, cower and fear this person entirely. All they want is to escape the punishment and make it stop.

If we can remove our emotions from the correction, we will achieve the results we want much more quickly and effectively. I know for some people this is easier said than done. We have frustration and anger building inside us and we often feel justified in punishing the dog. "How dare he chew my sofa? He knows better than that! I'm going to tan his hide!"

I hear statements like this a lot.

"He knows better." That's like saying a baby knows better than to soil their diaper. Like I said earlier, if your dog is not chewing, jumping, urinating in your house or stealing your food, he is denying his very nature. A dog will gladly do this for a person he respects, reveres, trusts and feels is his leader. He is *more* likely to exhibit these unwanted behaviors if he is fearful, threatened, abused or screamed at.

Can you imagine the stress of thinking someone might yell at you at any minute? If your dog has not associated his behavior with your yelling, then, in his mind, you are just randomly screaming at him. If he forgets the lesson because of extreme corrections, he is very likely to think his crazy owner just lashes out at will. However, if during his unwanted behavior he is corrected in a calm, authoritative way, which will mimic a dog's correction. He is very likely to learn what you want from him and adopt that behavior in the future.

Make the punishment fit the crime. Stick to the lesson at hand and keep it confined to a split second. The instant the correction is finished and your dog has complied, immediately go back to being his best friend. That's the way dogs handle their differences.

Aren't these simple, but amazing lessons for our own lives? A grudge never gets you anywhere. Holding on to anger and frustration only hurts the person who is angry and frustrated. My dogs have taught me so much about keeping a peaceful mind and a forgiving attitude

Have you ever really noticed the feeling of relief when you apologize to someone and they accept it? Isn't it a wonderful feeling when we reconcile and all of the bad feelings of a disagreement go away? Dogs go through this in a split second. They don't linger in their bad feelings.

In the years I have been training dogs, I have tried to carry this lesson into my every day life. When I have a disagreement with a person, I tend to address it head on, immediately. I go to the person in a calm, rational tone of voice. I get right to the point of the issue in a relaxed way. I try to sort it out with simple language and I don't beat around the bush. If I am wrong, I am the first to surrender and apologize. When the weight of that disagreement is lifted off of both of our shoulders, I move on and never look back at the perceived problem or transgression. It's now over for good.

I learned this way of being from dogs. I used to be a person who worried more, thought about negative things way too much and held onto resentments for way too long. I was only hurting myself. The more I worked with and studied dogs, I noticed how happy they could be. They don't worry like we do. Of course dogs are affected by the sad things they sometimes go through. They are changed by dysfunctional situations they are put in. However, a healthy, balanced dog is generally a happy dog. I believe this is, in large part, due to the way they handle conflict.

Imagine if you could let go of all resentment, all bad thoughts toward others or situations you couldn't control. If we could all live in the moment and just deal with the minute to minute living of life, imagine how happy we would be. Dogs are simply dealing with now, this minute. They don't project into the future and they don't live in the past. They just get on with the living of now.

I encourage you to put aside your thoughts of what your dog did wrong yesterday or might do wrong tomorrow. Try to focus on right now. Address his behavior today, this minute, and this second. Don't invest your correction with anger left over from the things he did yesterday or last week. Don't be mad about how much the item cost that he ruined or how much you might feel he is behaving badly to "personally" spite you. Try to see the behavior from your dog's point of view and correct on his level. Give him a correction he can get his head around. Make it simple and to the point so he can associate the moment, assimilate it and move on. Isn't that simple?

Our dogs teach us so much! If we pay attention, they offer a great philosophy and way to approach life. If we were able to give up our attachment to material things the way a dog can, we wouldn't care so much about the cost of the item the dog might have an accident on. Isn't it our fault, anyway, if we gave our dog access to something before he had learned the lesson reliably? If we placed value and importance more on our relationship with our dog and less on the inanimate object he destroyed, wouldn't life be happier?

The same goes for our relationships in general. How much closer would we feel to our family and friends if we had no grudges? If we held no resentments, wouldn't it be easier to be close, to bond with someone else and simply live in the moment? This is how your dog lives. He doesn't care about material things or perceived wrongs done to him. He just lives moment to moment. He starts fresh with everyone, giving second chance after second chance. Look at how joyful your dog is! I believe a big part of this joy is because he doesn't hold onto worries, grudges and resentment. He simply lives in the moment.

THE NOT SO SECRET LANGUAGE

Among the many ways dogs communicate with each other, there are three very specific tools they use to show dominance over another dog and to make corrections. I have implemented these and modified them just slightly to make them easy for a human to use. If you can master these three simple ways of communicating, it will forever change your relationship with your dog for the better.

Earlier, I have talked about the way in which a dog lives in the moment. His corrections happen in a split second and get right to the point. He doesn't mess around.

How, specifically, does he do this? He uses his body language, his tone of voice and his mouth.

Let's start with tone of voice.

When a dog doesn't like another dog's behavior, he finds a way, in his own language, to tell that dog to stop it. He doesn't say, "I'm sorry, Mr. Dog. You're standing a bit too close for my comfort. Can you please move back a couple of steps?" Ridiculous, right?

It seems absurd to think of one dog saying this to another. So, why is it we think it's perfectly normal to yell, "I told you to get off the couch!"

Of course, this sometimes works. Most likely, it's because the dog is overwhelmed by the sound, intimidated and feeling the need to flee the unpleasantness. Worse, he may even get so scared he growls or lashes out. When scared to the point they feel they have to defend themselves, a dog will lash out because of his survival instinct.

Some dogs are just so smart and adept at acclimating to our ridiculous human ways that they just learn what we want through trial and error. They study us closely and begin to figure out what it is we desire. They observe our words, body language and complicated communication tools until they get the general idea of our intent.

Wouldn't it be easier just to learn how your dog would do it?

Let's say your dog has just started to chew your table leg and you want him to stop. You could panic, run over, yelling all the way and drag him away by his collar. He will probably infer that you don't like what he is doing. He will also assume that you are overreacting, out of control and a little bit unstable. This is definitely not the behavior of a dog pack leader!

Your dog wants to follow a strong, calm, in control leader. He is drawn to pack leaders that lead in a relaxed but firm, quiet but effective style and demeanor. He is most likely to obey a leader that is clear in his commands.

A good pack leader makes the rules black and white. It's immediately clear what is right or wrong, good or bad, pleasant or unpleasant. There is no grey area in the establishment of rules and boundaries. The leader's wishes are clear and final.

Think of some leaders you know. The President? A policeman? A teacher? They get right to the point, take control of a situation and try to remain cool, calm and collected, right? They don't scream and yell and flail their arms around in a panic. Imagine if you went to see the doctor and he came into the exam room unsure, nervous, frustrated or out of control. Would you feel comfortable following his direction?

When a person studies to become a police officer, they are taught to arrive on the scene with an attitude of "Command Presence". In other words, they project an attitude of being in control. Their very presence exudes leadership, control and strength. It calms those around him and sends a message of safety and security. You don't see a police officer walking up to your car window to issue a citation and begin talking in baby talk. He doesn't offer you treats and beg you to comply. He uses a few words and he speaks with confidence and control. Once you are in compliance, the policeman can begin to relax his stance a little bit and give you a softer attitude. You show respect, he shows respect. See the relationship that begins to form? Mutual respect.

Your dog has the same instinct. He is much more likely to follow the commands of a person in charge and exhibiting the behaviors of a leader. This is a person he can get behind, feel safe and relinquish his control to.

When a dog wants his command to be followed, he is not concerned with words. He uses tools that are very specific. He uses the communication skills of an animal. Animals don't drag out the point of a conversation. They get right to the heart of the matter.

If he doesn't have words, what does your dog rely on?

Let's consider sound. He has a very specific tone of voice he uses when he means business. When he wants to say, "Stop it immediately!" he gives one, low, short, sharp bark. He does this once. He wants the behavior of the other dog to stop NOW! Many different barks mean many different things, but one, low, intense, percussive "Rowf!" means "STOP!"

By all means, you are welcome to simply imitate this sound. The word attached to it doesn't matter, initially. However, if you make the sound with a word attached, your dog will begin to learn this word.

Isn't that amazing?

He doesn't use words or even have the part of the brain that makes verbal language. Because he loves us, though, he reaches out and tries his best to acclimate and learn what we are saying. He will learn that word incredibly fast if you say it with the sound he already understands. He is trying to learn our language, the least we can do is learn a bit of his in return.

If you begin to make this sound attached to corrections, soon you will find yourself having to be less intense with the sound and relying on just the word more and more. You make it easier for your dog to make the transition to understanding us clearly. You can attach "No" or "Off" or "Stop" or "Quit". If the sound is right, the word matters a lot less.

I do suggest, though, that you pick a word and stick with it. It is not fair to your dog to constantly change it on him. He is trying so hard to please you, let's keep it consistent for his sake.

I use "No" for misbehavior, in general. You can use any word you are comfortable with. However, when it comes to jumping up on you or on the furniture, I recommend that you don't say "Down". When we teach our dog to lie down we use "Down" within that command. If we use the same word for a correction, it can be very confusing and stressful for your dog. You have yelled "DOWN!" when you wanted him off the couch. An hour later, you're saying "down" in a loving tone and hoping for a positive result. This is a common, but terrible mistake for a dog parent to make!

A lot of times, I use the word "Hey" for corrections. It is so versatile and I am less likely to use it for other things. It's unlikely that I will attach a command to "Hey". Therefore, it comes naturally to me in moments of displeasure with my dog. It's also less harsh than a lot of other choices.

Tone is everything. Volume is not. You should never have to yell or scream at your dog. The more volume you add, the further you are from your lesson. I see people get frustrated when their dog doesn't obey immediately. I watch them yell louder and louder, throw out more and more words and finally grab the dog and force him into behaving. All this does is intensify the problem.

Your dog hears at four to five times the level of intensity that we hear. When you yell or make too much sound, your dog becomes overwhelmed.

Imagine you are in a tense situation. Maybe you are arguing with someone or somebody is displeased with you. Suddenly, someone blows an air horn in your ear. Maybe they turn up a stereo really loud. Is all of this intense sound helping the situation? It definitely is not.

Watch dogs playing with each other. Except for play barks, there is not a lot of sound exchanged. Everything happens relatively quietly. They certainly don't yell and they definitely don't use loud words.

Calm intensity is the key. Have you seen a child throw a tantrum? Have you seen his mother get frustrated and angry? What happens to the child? They get upset, scared, cry. Sometimes the tantrum gets worse. The situation escalates. It certainly doesn't help a child to learn a lesson by being yelled at. In most cases, the most effective thing to do is to become calm. A parent doesn't get down in the floor with his child and scream and kick with him. He gets the child's attention, looks him in the eye and calmly, but intensely, says, "Calm down!"

The principle is the same with your dog. If you become calm, in control and intense, that is energy your dog is very likely to comply with. That is the energy an alpha dog would come at him with in an out of control situation. A pack leader controls his follower by example, not by getting down on the dog's level and losing control with him. He brings the other dog to his level of stillness.

Your dog will reflect your energy and behavior. If you build the kind of leader/follower, parent/child relationship with your dog I am talking about, he will have no choice but to begin to reflect your behavior and energy level. Dogs are built to follow and emulate their leader. It is the way nature designed it. That's why I suggest we work with nature and not against it.

TOUCH/BITES

The second tool a dog uses when making a correction is extremely effective. When a short burst of sound isn't enough, when a look doesn't work and the other dog doesn't comply, his next tactic is to use a very specific kind of bite. Starting from the very beginning of his life, a puppy's mother will use a targeted kind of nip that tells the dog in no uncertain terms he should immediately stop what he is doing. Of course, a mother dog doesn't want to hurt her baby. She only wants to interrupt his behavior and make it stop.

Just like with kids, sometimes a warning is enough. Sometimes all it takes is a look or a sound to make them stop what they're doing. However, there comes a time when you have to get a dog's attention another way. Sometimes a dog is fixated on what he is doing, lost in thought or ramped up so much he can't think straight. Sometimes he bites too hard, plays too rough or is doing something dangerous. This requires a serious kind of correction that the dog will remember and associate with his behavior.

When a mother dog decides to use her teeth, she is very controlled and specific about it. Her intent is not to hurt the dog or his feelings.

She basically wants to "snap him out of it". She strikes fast, like a snake. She will pinch a bit of skin in her teeth, in a very targeted way. She wants to create a moment of shock, not to cause great pain or injury. From the outside, this can look scary. If you are not experienced and haven't seen many dog corrections, it can seem like the mother dog is attacking her puppy. If this is a normal correction, though, it will be over quickly.

The moment usually goes something like this. A puppy is nursing too hard, playing too rough or some other unwanted behavior. His mother turns, in an instant, gives the low, sharp bark and lunges at the puppy with her mouth. Her teeth very decisively pinch a bit of skin or she firmly touches the puppy with her muzzle. The puppy yelps, often acting like it's the end of the world. He, of course, immediately stops whatever he was doing. His mother backs off immediately. The puppy goes on to something else and the mother relaxes her demeanor. The lesson is over and they are back to being loving in no time.

This is a miraculous moment of nature! If done correctly, corrections don't have to happen over and over. Once a puppy knows that the consequence for his behavior is swift and unpleasant, he doesn't really want to repeat the lesson. Would you? However, if the mother were to give the correction weakly or muddy it up with extra sound and confusing messages, the pup would have a lot more trouble absorbing the lesson. One firm, reasonable, authoritative correction beats fifty half-hearted punishments.

This is one of the hardest lessons for some people. Of course, no one wants to hurt his or her dog. Nobody wants to hurt his or her feelings, either. However, every child, human or animal, needs guidance, boundaries and rules to get through life. We are not fully loving our dog if we are not providing discipline and structure for him. You wouldn't send your child out into the world without teaching him the good with the bad. He needs to be prepared.

I know what you're thinking… "I don't want to have to bite my dog!"

I'm not saying you should. I don't think any of us wants a mouth full of fur. There is a very specific way to recreate the feeling of a mother dog's nip. If we can learn to touch our dogs in a quick, slightly "rude" sort of way, this can feel like a bite to them.

Imagine a bully coming up to you and poking you in the shoulder. It doesn't really hurt. You feel it, though, and it feels unpleasant. This touch has an energy behind it that is uncomfortable. A bully wants to make his point and make sure you know he is more dominant than you are. If he's going to poke you in the shoulder, he's not going to do it weakly. How he touches you is going to tell you a lot about who he is. If he accosts you and pokes you in a "rude" way, you're going to feel intimidated. This is the type of poke we are trying to mimic.

You have to be very careful! You have to modify your touch for each specific dog. You're not going to give a little Yorkshire Terrier a poke with the same intensity you would a wild and boisterous Labrador Retriever. I always say the punishment needs to fit the crime. Dogs have their own level of touch that works. I believe in making the least amount of correction necessary to achieve the result you want. So, if you have a sensitive dog, your touch may have hardly any intensity at all. If you have a wild dog, you may find yourself intensifying your poke to a stronger level.

Always apply this method to a part of the dog that is not going to hurt him. You NEVER want to poke your dog in the throat or face or anywhere sensitive. I recommend the shoulder. Poking your dog with your finger assertively, but not mean, is very effective. It's not necessarily the location of the little jab that is important. It's how you apply it. If you do it to a part of the body that hurts the dog, you have lost your lesson and betrayed your dog's trust. Not only that, it's mean!

You never want to do anything that will damage your dog's trust. A swift nip to a non-painful part of the body, then ending the lesson in a split second is a sure way to build trust. This is exactly how his mother did it and he will associate your method of correction with that period of his development. Who does a puppy trust more than his mother?

A quick tug of the leash achieves the same result. When we use the leash like a "firm touch" we can recreate that nip feeling. Pulling is not the same. When you pull on your dog's leash or he pulls against you for a prolonged period, you are actually teaching him to pull.

Dogs have something called opposition reflex. When you pull on them, their reflexive instinct is to pull against whatever it is that's pulling them. Think of Huskies and other sled dogs. They are taught to pull by pulling back against them. They have an instinct for it. But a quick tug and release, then putting the leash back to a loose, relaxed position, mimics the feeling of a bite. It's a correction.

I know a lot of people are afraid of hurting their dog's feelings. I assure you, if you are applying the lessons correctly, kindly, with restraint, you are not hurting your dog's feelings. It hurts more when the lessons are prolonged.

When we yell or go on and on with our frustration or anger or punishment, that begins to take a toll on your dog. Have you ever done something wrong and somebody just won't let it go? They talk on and on about it, making you feel worse and worse. Now, imagine you don't know exactly what they are saying. Wouldn't that just make you feel upset and confused?

If you can learn to correct like a dog, your dog is actually going to love you for it! You are providing leadership he can understand and relate to. You are speaking his language and giving him a structure and discipline he can rely on and grow from. You are actually deepening your relationship with your dog when you correct him in his native language. You're helping him learn about boundaries and expectations. Isn't that beautiful?

Just the way a child later in life thanks his parents for teaching him hard lessons early on, your dog will thank you for being a firm but fair leader. He actually craves the kind of discipline he can get his head around. Once he understands and complies with you, you will begin to see him drawn to you. Dogs adore their leaders. They want to please a strong, firm, but loving leader. When we find this place of balance with our dog, our relationship blossoms and becomes something bigger and better than if we just pour on affection all the time.

BODY LANGUAGE

All day long your dog is speaking to you. If you watch closely, he is telling you an array of things simply by the way he carries himself. Body language is one of the foremost ways dogs have conversations with each other. They have no trouble interpreting what other dogs are trying to say to them. It's second nature.

When you try to understand your dog's language, it's not always easy for a person to interpret. Unless you have taken the time to study your dog, you might miss some of the subtleties he is putting out there. At any given time, he is telling anyone listening exactly how he is feeling, what he is thinking about and what kind of mood he is in.

Because your dog doesn't have the advantage of human words, we have to rely on other aspects of his language to begin to understand him. A strong alpha dog will hold himself tall and strong, yet relaxed and at ease. He will enter an area like he belongs there and sort of "take over" with his body language. He moves like he is confident, he approaches other dogs unafraid and he doesn't hesitate to do whatever he wants to.

Often, because of his manner of holding himself, an alpha dog doesn't have to do much else to prove his position. Other dogs read his confident body language and simply give him the role of leadership. They turn their bodies away from him, lower their head and give him an area of space around him until he decides they can approach. It's all done silently, but clearly.

In our human world, we often do a variation of this behavior without even being aware of it. We come in contact with a person of authority or confidence and we defer to them. They put out an air of calm and control. They actually help us to ease our worry by their demeanor. A boss, a policeman or a celebrity might convey a strong, but relaxed manner. This actually makes people *want* to follow them. They chose to defer to this person's authority, simply by the aura the person is presenting.

When a child is unsure or insecure, his parents will try to comfort him with more than just words. By showing that they are in control, they are telling their child that he has nothing to fear. They are there to protect him. Though they don't have to say it with words, the message is, "If something goes wrong, my Mom and Dad will handle it!"

That is exactly what happens in a dog's world. A dog's deepest desire is to know who is in control. Who will handle it if something goes wrong? If your dog were in a wild pack of dogs, he would look for a leader that would keep predators away and make sure nobody gets killed. This leadership starts with a sense of strength and calm.

One of the beautiful benefits of providing this leadership is that you will notice your dog beginning to relax. If your dog is not a born alpha dog (and most are not) he will be grateful to you for taking responsibilities off of his shoulders. You can imagine how stressful it would be to put a five-year-old child in charge of the mortgage, the car payment and the electric bill. That's how your dog must feel when he sees that no one in your house is in firm control. When you lead him, you *are* loving him.

Let's say you've just adopted a dog that comes to you with fears and neuroses brought with him from a previous, bad situation. The first thing most of us want to do is hug and squeeze and love all over the dog. Imagine how overwhelming this would be to an animal that might never have experienced this. Besides, it's not the natural way any dog greets another. If I just met you and put my hands in your face and picked you up, I think you might be more than just a little bit uncomfortable!

The best way to meet a new dog is to demonstrate a strong body language and an indifferent attitude. We don't try to force the dog out of his unsure state of mind. We approach without making eye contact, little or no sound and remain calm in our demeanor. Allow the dog to investigate and discover you at his own pace. Don't try to make him like you. We are not trying to coax him out of his shell. We don't want to talk him into a different way of being. We are allowing a quiet, calm, emotionally indifferent environment in which to figure us out on his own. He is more likely to build trust and relaxation when he decides to feel those things by himself. We can't force him to feel that way.

As the dog learns we are strong leaders who always lead him into safe situations, he begins to trust. If this is done properly and sensitively, dogs tend to recover much more quickly than human beings. They don't hold grudges or dwell on the past. People tend to hold onto past traumas much longer than dogs do. When properly led out of it, dogs tend to turn over their issues to their pack leader. That leader should demonstrate why the dog no longer needs to lean on his own neurotic behavior.

Think of a person drowning. That person does not want someone to come along and jump in the water with him. He doesn't want someone standing there; sweetly telling him everything is going to be all right. He wants someone strong to jump in the water and rescue him. He wants to be pulled to shore. He doesn't want you to come down to his level; he wants you to bring him up to your level.

No dog wants to live in his own neuroses and fear. However, he doesn't know any other way to cope. He begins to think that cowering, hiding and slinking around with lower body language will keep him safe.

If he has hidden under a table and then ended up being safe, he can start to believe that it is his behavior that has kept him that way. Later, this neurosis can grow into fear biting, barking and other behaviors that he learns work to keep others at bay. Each time a person backs off or coos, "It's okay. It's alright" the dog is learning that this sort of behavior achieves great results. It gets him exactly what he wants. People either give him his space or they encourage him in his behavior by inadvertently praising him.

Since dogs don't grasp full sentences and paragraphs, they key in to the sounds associated with the words. Think how similar the sound of praise is to the sound of sympathy. "It's okay, it's alright," are said with the same tone of voice as, "Good boy, good job!"

How confusing is that?

If you are a creature that never uses words and you rely on the tone of the message to understand, this can cause a lot of chaos in your world.

It's important to assess each dog individually. You want to find the level of intensity that is appropriate for your dog. We don't want to overwhelm him, but we want to find a level of approach, where the dog understands you are a leader, but you are not out to hurt him. It's all unspoken. Our goal is to present the truth of who we are.

How are you approaching?

How are you feeling?

Are you calm and without emotion?

Are you relaxed?

Are you ramped up and frustrated?

Are you afraid?

Whatever state of emotion you are in, I guarantee your dog will read it.

When any person, dog or other animal enters a room, we all make an instant judgment as to what they are all about.

Are they tough?

Are they timid?

Are they in control?

Are they frantic?

Safe, dangerous?

Old, young?

Kind, mean?

What are you presenting to others when you arrive?

What has your dog decided about you before you ever open your mouth?

This is the core of communicating with your dog. This is the very essence of animals understanding other animals. Ask yourself, "What am I presenting myself to be before I ever speak a word?"

If you put forth the energy of a person who is strong and authoritative, yet loving and trustworthy, your dog is likely to worship you! Dogs adore their leaders and are eager to please them. They bond deeply to a dominant but fair pack leader. They want to do almost anything that leader expects of them. It is their nature. They crave a reliable pack leader.

Body language is one of the clearest and most effective tools your dog uses to demonstrate this strength. There are many subtleties a dog looks for when identifying a dominant dog. I encourage you to look for these behaviors and start to incorporate them in your own way of interacting with your own dog.

Standing tall is the easiest. Choosing not to slump over, not to bend to your dog immediately upon entering a room and keeping your posture up all send a message of dominance. That doesn't mean you should never bend over or get down on your dog's level. It just means you can use this tool when you want to display dominance. If you are aware of the clear message this sends to your dog, you will see how powerful it is.

Many times our dog is doing this to us and we don't even recognize it. They add another element to this behavior that other dogs read immediately. Dominant dogs will often crowd another dog. They will stand too close and move into another dog's space until that dog moves. When one dog moves in and the other moves away, they have just had a conversation. "I am the leader, you are the follower. I am stronger, you are weaker. I am dominant, you are submissive."

Have you ever been petting a dog and another dog walks in between you and that dog? He shoves the other dog aside and demands that you pet him instead. He has just demonstrated dominant behavior toward both of you. If you don't correct it, you are sending the message that you don't disagree with him. If he gets away with it, then he is reinforced in his position as dominant dog. If you pet him every time he demands it or steals your attention from another dog, you are sending a message of encouragement. He has just dominated both you and the other dog and is being rewarded for it.

Many people think this is cute. They think their dog loves them so much they just have to be near them. They have to hog all the affection because they are so closely bonded to us or jealous of other dogs or people. This behavior can turn bad very quickly.

How would you feel if you were in line at a restaurant and someone stepped in front of you? They never look you in the eye or apologized. Then, they stand too close to you with their back turned. When they were about to be seated, they asked you for money to pay for their food. Ridiculous, right? Then why should it be okay for our dog to act this way?

Most of us in a moment like this would be assertive and say something. We would be firm, but fair. We don't start by yelling or fighting. We simply say something about the rudeness. We disagree with the behavior in a firm but fair way. That's how I suggest looking at your dog when he is crowding you. We're going to "disagree" with the behavior.

Sometimes this behavior begins to grow until the dog develops a neurotic addiction to our affection. I have seen countless dogs that just can't get enough petting and cuddling. When we stop petting, the dog starts pushing with his nose, whining, shoving with his body and sometimes worse.

This is sort of like a child who finishes an ice cream cone and immediately wants more. We say no and the child starts whining and complaining. If we give in, we are teaching the child that if he just whines long enough, he'll get more ice cream. By setting a limit on the amount of ice cream a child eats, we are actually loving him and looking out for his best interest.

If a dog is simply being a little bit needy, that can be relatively harmless. Sometimes it doesn't go any further than a few whines or nose shoves. However, a dominant dog with the potential for aggression can turn these situations into something much more threatening.

I worked with a family that had a German Shepherd named Zeus, who was about three-years-old and had recently begun to act aggressively toward the mother of the family. When I arrived, I could see the problem immediately. The father was very authoritative in his leadership. He was quick and sharp with his commands and firm with his expectations. As soon as Zeus obeyed, the dad became sweet and affectionate.

The children were relatively indifferent toward Zeus. However, when he crowded them or followed too close or bothered them, they told him "no" in a strong, clear way. Zeus complied and the kids had a relatively balanced relationship with him.

The mom, on the other hand, was very passive in her demeanor. She was extremely soft-spoken, used a lot of words, a higher tone of voice and rarely corrected Zeus. When she wanted him to do something, she asked politely and used a sweet, soft voice, requesting Zeus to listen...if he felt like it. Needless to say, Zeus took full advantage of this situation.

While I was talking with the family, Zeus calmly walked over to Mom and slowly climbed into her lap. This is often not even noticeable when we're dealing with a small lap dog. However, Zeus was a full-grown German Shepherd! The mom responded by hugging him, loving on him and showing great affection. In fact, she told me she loved him climbing all over her. To her, this represented love and affection. However, in the dog's mind this was very different. It was not a show of love, but a show of control. I assure you he was controlling the situation.

When I stepped over to get Zeus off the chair, he growled and showed his teeth. Mom responded to this by sweetly saying, "It's okay! You're alright! Shhh!" Of course, this was immediately interpreted by Zeus as praise for his aggressive behavior.

The mother told me that Zeus did this with the children, as well. He climbed into their laps and if Mom told him to get down, he growled and bared his teeth at her. However, when Dad told him to get down with one word "down!" Zeus immediately complied.

Can you see the bigger picture here?

Some of these little offenses are very subtle and if we are not looking for them, we don't even know it's going on. A lot of people think it's cute or lovable for their dog to demand attention. Often, it doesn't go any further than simple "rudeness". However, some dogs that are prone to neurotic or aggressive behavior can start small. They begin exhibiting small infractions like shoving, crowding or climbing into laps without an invitation. When no one corrects it, they mentally file that moment away as an accomplishment. They begin to see themselves as getting away with something. They think they've just moved up a notch in the pack order.

With Zeus, I began working with the family to send messages of leadership throughout the day. They should be telling him who the boss is at times other than when he is testing his boundaries. If he believes you are his pack leader when things are calm and not much is going on, he is more likely to bring that belief with him into a confrontational situation.

If your dog is prone to being assertive, small infractions can be the beginning of a bigger problem. Often, this kind of dog will then move on to more serious offenses. If he can get away with a shove, maybe next it's climbing on you or the furniture. Maybe he takes over some of your possessions or marks his territory. Another warning sign is growling or snarling, showing his teeth or refusing to obey your commands. These can start small and before you know it, he's biting, lunging and out of control.

I don't mean to scare you! I just want to warn you that these behaviors are so much easier to correct at the earliest sign of the first offense. Once a stockpile of bad incidents begins to add up in the dog's mind, it's so much harder to bring him back to square one.

This goes for all obedience training. Behaviors are so much easier to correct at level one, the first small infraction, than level four, five or ten. Try to be your dog's leader in the beginning before it gets out of control. Don't wait until bad behavior becomes unmanageable. Nip it in the bud.

The Zeus story had a happy ending. The mom got it right away and with some simple adjustments in her every day behavior, Zeus turned around immediately. In fact, before I left after one session, he was listening to her commands and she could easily get him to jump down out of her children's laps.

In the same way a dog uses crowding and pushiness to test your authority, we can use it in reverse to tell him we are the boss.

Try walking into your dog's space until he moves. You can actually herd your dog around simply by blocking him and moving in the direction you want him to move. You shouldn't always have to grab his collar, bend over, and wrestle with him. In fact, this kind of pulling and pushing actually stimulates your dog's instinct to pull and push against you. Remember, the scientific term for this is opposition reflex. They oppose your action of pulling by pulling in the other direction. It's their instinct.

If you want to teach a dog to pull on a leash, pull back. That is the surest way to get him to pull against you. Picture a pack of sled dogs. They can pull a person on a fully loaded sled for miles. Your dog can certainly pull you down the street. The trick is not to continuously pull. You want to tug and release to make a correction. If you can avoid pulling on the collar at all, that would be the ideal. Dogs in the wild don't use collars. You definitely never see one dog pulling another around with a leash. They use a language that is instantly more effective.

Sometimes your arms are full of groceries or you are cooking dinner. Your dog gets under your feet. Simply move into his space, block him from dodging around you and herd him back to where you want him. Don't let him avoid what you want from him. You are the leader. He has to follow your will. Just walk forward into his space until he moves. Once he complies, you can back off and return to what you were doing. If he challenges you, do it again until he gets the message. You are the authority figure, here, and you make the rules.

You have just had a non-verbal conversation with your dog. You have just said, "I am the leader, you are the follower." If your dog complied with this exercise, he has just told you, "No problem! I surrender to your authority and I get what you're trying to tell me."

Dogs have an incredible sense of spatial awareness. When someone else moves into his or her spatial bubble or personal space, they feel it and react accordingly. Some dogs get nervous, some get annoyed, but the great majority simply comply and move away. This is a conversation they clearly understand.

All of the words in the world will not get this point across as quickly and effectively as this simple motion. This is a language your dog already speaks. It transcends all verbal conversation and conveys a sense of order to the pack. As soon as your dog complies, you can go right back to love and affection. "Good boy!" He has just made a great choice. When your dog is in that state of mind, he is eager to please and happy to follow your authority. While his mind is in this state, feel free to be as affectionate and loving as you want to be. This is the time to pour on the love!

PRAISE AND AFFECTION

When your dog is exhibiting behavior that you like and desire, that is when we want to reinforce his behavior with affection. When your dog is exhibiting unwanted behavior, we switch to our dominant, strong self. It becomes so easy when we understand how truly simple it is. If we make things black or white, right or wrong, good or bad, then our dog has a concept he can get his mind around. We are giving our dog a clear opportunity to do the right thing because we have made it simple enough for him to understand.

When you are being affectionate toward your dog, you are reinforcing whatever state of mind he is in at that moment. If he is afraid or aggressive and you say sweetly, "It's okay. You're alright," he hears your tone of voice saying, "Good boy! I love that behavior! Please be more afraid and aggressive!"

Remember, words are not a dog's first choice of communication. He is used to hearing soft, sweet tones of voice when he is being praised for good behavior. He is less likely to understand the meaning of the sentences you are saying to him. So, remove the words and what you are left with is a voice that he associates with good behavior.

You might as well be saying, "I love it when you're neurotic! Do more of that! Could you please be more neurotic?"

Dogs don't hold a grudge. Once the lesson is over, it's over. They don't prolong the anger and resentment. Dogs snap or snarl, one of them wins the moment, the other surrenders. Once the moment passes, they are on to the next thing. They don't sit around dwelling on the past offense. Imagine how much happier our lives would be if we could learn this one, simple lesson!

Of course, there are always exceptions. You might have a dog that has gone a little further down the path. He is now moving up the aggression ladder. You walk into his space, he turns his head to the side and growls, giving you a dirty look. This is a dog telling you, "No! I don't surrender to your authority!" This is a bratty kid. Unfortunately, it's a bratty kid with a dangerous weapon; sharp teeth! I recommend if you get this kind of response that you don't escalate the situation. Don't yell, don't keep moving forward, and don't try frantically to make him submit. However, don't back down, either. Simply stand your ground, silently and patiently. The first to walk away is the submissive on. Make sure that it is your dog that walks and not you! Then, get professional help from a reputable dog behavior expert.

Above all else, in a situation like this, remain calm. Take a deep breath and think about other things. Whatever it takes for you to relax and stand perfectly still. It might take one minute or it might take five. Whatever it takes, be calm, be patient and stand still. This is one piece in the puzzle of reclaiming your position as leader of your pack. Dogs take these moments very seriously and so should you. When we downplay it or fearfully slink away or decide to deal with it later, we are showing weakness and our dog will remember it.

However, if we keep moving forward or try to grab the dog, yell, get angry, frustrated or any number of emotional responses, we are demonstrating a lack of control. Your dog will see that you don't have the ability to restrain your emotions and, therefore, you are weak. This sends a subliminal message that he can "take you". It also throws gasoline on an already smoldering fire. When you calm down and relax, your dog will begin to reflect that state of mind.

Affection is not the cure for an unbalanced dog. Human nature is to "love the problem away." Many people believe that with enough love and affection, a dog will get past its problems. This is simply not true. In addition, rules, discipline and structure ARE love and affection. If you adopted a child with a criminal history, loving affection would not be his only cure. He would need much more to have a well-rounded life.

It is in an alpha dog's best interest to control his pack and his own decisions. If we could all be the decision makers in our home, I suppose we would all try to take on that role. However, life doesn't work that way. When we live with others we have to compromise, follow rules and show respect. These rules are better made by a human with the ability to reason. It's not so great when the dog rules the house!

I absolutely do NOT recommend a confrontation with an aggressive dog! Avoid it at all costs. Don't tackle this by yourself. You need professional help, if the situation has reached this stage.

When a dog has reached an aggressive, confrontational stage, he is beyond simple corrections. He needs to have an entire psychological shift to know he is not the boss. He needs to be rehabilitated out of this way of being. This is not always easily accomplished without professional guidance. People tend to approach situations like this with frustration, anger, tension or fear. Sometimes it's all of the above! This attitude will definitely NOT help you gain control.

I once worked with a woman who had a wild and aggressive Chihuahua. The dog was extremely territorial and lashed out at anyone who tried to get near his possessions, food or his "person". He believed his owner was actually controlled by him! The roles were completely reversed. His "mom" would yell and pull his leash and try to control him through frustration and screaming. She kept telling me, "I'm calm. I'm in control. I'm not afraid." However, everything she was presenting said the opposite.

This little Chihuahua sensed that his mom was not in control. She was nervous about the dog's behavior, but he didn't know that was the reason. All he saw was that his mother had lost control of her emotions whenever a person walked in the room. She may have thought she was hiding her emotions, but dogs are extremely intuitive.

From the dog's point of view, here comes a stranger. Mom gets nervous. The message being sent to the dog is people are something to be feared. Mom doesn't control the situation and she certainly is not acting like a dog pack leader. Therefore, the dog assumes it is his job to take care of this thing that's making his mom nervous. The dog clearly sees himself as the strong one in this scenario.

Most of the time, this behavior starts small. It goes unnoticed or isn't corrected. Each time the dog lashes out, people back off. It works! Then, his human Mom starts by telling him, "It's okay, it's alright!" This encourages him in his tantrum. Long after the dog is in a frenzy and can't think straight, people begin yelling, "No!"

When you think of situations like this from the dog's point of view, it seems kind of ridiculous, doesn't it? So often, we apply human logic to the circumstances. It's time to start approaching it like a dog.

When a dog is lunging on the end of a leash, off leash in front of us or between an owner and a perceived threat, he is in a body position of leadership over the person standing behind him. If he sees nobody between him and the approaching thing that he is unsure of, he is going to take it upon himself to make his own decisions about those things.

A nervous, unsure leader will find a neurotic way of dealing with things. Would you want to follow a leader in this state of mind? When you are yelling and frustrated and frantic, your dog is looking at you exactly the same way you look at him when he behaves that way.

Would you be more likely to respect someone who is still and strong or someone lunging and making loud sounds?

Don't try to fight fire with fire. If your dog is loud and you try to out shout him, you are only escalating the situation. If your dog is lunging and out of control, pulling him and struggling in a frustrated state of mind is like throwing gasoline on a fire. It only makes things so much worse.

Start by positioning yourself between your dog and the threatening situation. Face him and move into his space. Be calm and display control. Help him to understand that he belongs behind you. You will be the one to let him know how to feel about this person. You will be the one making the decisions about this situation.

Sitting, being calm and submitting to your authority are the perfect position for your dog to be in while meeting a new person. If you have control and are in front, then your dog has a safe place from which to assess the situation. He can see how you treat people from a safe vantage point. He will be able to slowly realize nobody is getting hurt and nothing bad is happening.

If you begin yelling to rise above your dog's barking, you are losing. If you are hitting, jerking on the leash or pulling, you are losing. If you are frustrated, angry or impatient, you are losing. Leadership is often a battle of wills and attitudes, but it is done with calm. If a two-year-old is screaming at you, you don't scream back. You quietly but firmly get him to calm down by bringing him down to your calm way of being. You need to be your dog's "rock". Be someone he can feel safe relying on and turning over his trust and safety to. Then, watch how his behavior blossoms. Dogs reflect their leaders. Ask yourself, "What kind of leader am I?"

When your dog begins to comply, that is when you can begin to give affection. I suggest that your praise be calm and with your voice, only, at this point. You don't have to bend over and pet him. He understands you without gushing and rubbing all over him. A calm, simple, "Good boy!" goes a long way. You don't want to get him so excited that he immediately ramps up again. Calm creates calm, quiet creates quiet and relaxation creates relaxation.

TRAIN WHEN IT DOESN'T MATTER

I tell all of my clients to "train when it doesn't matter". We should be teaching our dogs when there is nothing at stake. We shouldn't wait until something goes wrong or there is a battle of wills before we try to train. We should train when we aren't busy or rushed. We should train when nothing else is going on. We shouldn't wait for a chaotic crisis to try and give lessons.

We should be teaching our dogs every day, sometimes even unconsciously. Simply by our demeanor, tone of voice and way of being we are teaching our dog, whether we know it or not. If we slouch around, speak in a negative tone, demonstrate weakness, yell, whine or never show authority, little-by-little our dogs are absorbing this. They watch us intently picking up thousands of subtle messages just by the way we live.

Those of you who have children know how they are like little sponges. One day they say something or do something completely out of nowhere and we think, "Where did they learn that?" Sometimes our dog comes up with a behavior that seems completely foreign to us and we think exactly the same thing.

If we are conscientious parents, of humans or dogs, we try to be aware of the unspoken messages we are sending. We don't cuss in front of our children (hopefully!) because we are aware of the effect this has on them. However, we will do all sorts of things in front of our dog because we think he doesn't "get it". If you think your child is watching your every move, I guarantee your dog is just as perceptive. He has nowhere to go, no place to be. He doesn't go to school or work. He's got no dinner date or plans for an out of town vacation.

Your dog lives in your house waiting for you to lead the way. Any trips he takes elsewhere are because of you. Anything he is exposed to is completely up to you. Therefore, he has nothing better to do than size you up, look for ways to get what he wants from you and try to get your attention.

This is exactly why we should be teaching at times when nothing else is going on. In the same way a child has to make his bed, go to school and do his homework, your dog needs a purpose. He needs things to do. I hear people all the time who say, "He has a big back yard. He can run around all day doing whatever he wants to." That is like dropping your child off at an empty school and hoping he learns algebra. It's not very well thought out.

Structure means a lot to a dog. Having a routine that stays relatively the same each day is comforting to him. He likes it when breakfast happens at a similar time, when we go out, when we play, etc. When that changes all the time, it's more difficult for him to know what is expected of him. Doesn't this sound a lot like a child?

This doesn't mean that you have to always carve out a huge chunk of time for dog lessons. I am very aware that we all have lives and schedules and jobs and more. In fact, I have been known to be a bit of a slacker in the dog parenting department! This can be especially true if we have very well behaved dogs. They can be so calm and quiet that we almost forget to help them fulfill their needs.

Once you get in a routine with your dog, teaching and interacting just become a simple, beautiful part of your day. We don't have to say, "At 5:30, we are going to begin obedience lessons. At 5:45, we will play and at 6:00 we eat."

Instead, I believe it's easier to incorporate a lot of little interactions throughout the day. Let's say you're making breakfast. You're waiting for the coffee to brew or an egg to cook. Take that moment and ask your dog to sit. Maybe you'd rather throw a ball for him to retrieve. You could create a trick that only happens at breakfast. In this simple little moment, you have just taught a lesson, interacted and bonded with your dog. You haven't had to plan a thing or interrupt your day in any way.

I like to talk to my dogs (or even sing…don't tell anybody!) while I'm doing other things. I can be folding laundry or doing the dishes and all the while I'm having a conversation or saying their names. Of course, they don't get all the words. It is simply the sound of my voice, hearing their names and feeling that connection that not only fills them up inside, but it does a whole lot for me, too!

We can take advantage of the silliest little moments to connect to our dog. Singing, silly voices and baby talk are part of the joy of having a dog. The beautiful thing is, we don't have to be embarrassed. They don't judge us and certainly can't tell anybody how ridiculously we behave. In fact, they will be just as ridiculous right along with us!

Having a dog in the family should be a joy. It shouldn't have to feel like work. That's why I encourage people to find their own way of fitting their dog into what they are already doing. Many times, I've been on the phone while throwing the ball for my dogs. I had a Shepherd/Beagle mix named Annie for seventeen years. She would chase and retrieve a ball until you were worn out. I had to be careful not to let her exhaust herself! I would get on the phone and sit with her in the yard throwing the ball, petting her and having a great time without ever interrupting what I had to get done. It's so easy!

I like to take my dogs in the car with me. Sometimes, I'm not really going anywhere exciting. If I know I'm going to the drive-thru at the bank or to get fast food, why can't the dogs ride along with me? It's sort of a passive way of allowing them to be mentally stimulated while I get my errands done. Of course, I NEVER leave my dogs unattended in a car! Especially not in the heat or extreme cold! You wouldn't leave your child alone in a car, don't leave your dog, either.

These are just a few ideas and I'm sure you can think of many more. It's not a substitute for spending time with your dog and giving him your undivided attention. He deserves that kind of interaction as much as you do. However, these are just a few ways we can help to enrich our dog's life without changing much about our routine at all.

OBEDIENCE

Learning how to behave around guests, lie down, sit or stay are all separate and apart from your dog's physical and psychological needs. We have to spend some time focused on these and teach them thoroughly so they become a part of our dog's way of life.

Sit, especially, is so important. It is so useful in the human world. It is a behavior you can call upon to substitute bad behavior. It also becomes a command to get your dog to comply and tune in to your authority. I think it's essential.

The sit command is sort of like rebooting your computer. Dogs can really only focus on one thought at a time. They are not multi-taskers. They don't eat dinner while thinking, "I can't wait to play out in the yard." They focus on the task at hand. That's why substituting a thought about sitting can clear their head from thinking about other bad behaviors. It gives them something active to do instead of jumping, running, chewing, etc.

I have seen countless dogs go from frantic running and jumping to instant calm when given the "sit" command. Instead of making their own decisions and being scattered in a hundred directions, they now have an activity. They are actively complying with something their owner told them to do. This also sets the leader/follower relationship instantly in place. It provides structure, discipline and a place to look for what to do next.

What amazes me, in all my years of teaching, is how many people pass up these simple lessons. They just expect their dogs to know what to do without a plan. They turn their dog loose in the house and hope everything goes well. That is pretty ridiculous. Why should your dog just automatically know how to act in a human home? That's like hoping a child just figures out how to feed himself, use the bathroom or do math!

Let's use door manners as an example.

I go to homes all the time where the dogs are completely unruly and out of control at the door. They are barking and jumping all over a guest, the owners are yelling and pulling on the dog's collar and everyone is getting more and more frustrated and out of control.

Then, the owners look at me bewildered. "See? They're out of control? What's wrong with them?"

"What have you done to teach them how to behave?" I say.

"Well, when people come to the door, we pull them back and yell 'no'."

There is so much wrong with this answer!

First, it implies that they wait until someone is at the door to begin teaching the dog how they are expected to behave. That's like waiting until someone is ready to take their SAT test in high school before teaching them basic math. It's absurd!

To begin with, put your dog on a leash. This will help him to stay focused and not get distracted. It will also give you access to make a correction. Bring your dog to the door and have him sit, a few feet away. Step between the door and your dog and face him, with your back to the door. The leash should always be loose, except when making a quick correction. When everyone is calm and under control, knock on the door. Of course, your dog will probably react. Correct him immediately and put him back in a sit position. If he is being difficult, a quick leash correction, a step into his space and a firm, "SIT!" should do the trick. Return to knocking on the door.

We are going to repeat this behavior, slowly adding turning the knob, ringing the doorbell and knocking. It might take one minute or it might take five, but I assure you, if you remain calm and in control, your dog will eventually comply.

This begins to desensitize the dog to the sounds and actions of the door. Until we do this, the door only rings or knocks when someone is coming over. Therefore, to the dog, the doorbell means excitement. If we do it again and again when things are boring, the door becomes less and less exciting. Do this twice a day for no more than a few minutes and I guarantee, in a very short time, your dog will be easily falling into the behavior.

Before this lesson, the sounds of the door represent action. Something is happening or maybe there's danger. After several lessons, it all becomes no big deal. In fact, your dog might actually become bored with it all. Then, when we add a real guest, the dog knows what is expected of him. Before the lesson, how should he know? He's just being an excited dog!

Of course, when real people arrive, it adds a new exciting element. But control is so much easier to achieve once the dog is let in on the program. If they have been shown what is expected of them, we are halfway down the path when a guest comes over.

It seems logical, right?

This philosophy applies to all aspects of your dog's life. Train the behavior you want before you put your dog in the position of needing to know it. It might seem obvious, but you'd be surprised how many people don't grasp this simple concept. They just expect their dog to come "prepackaged" and know what they need to know. Why should they?

This is especially true of puppies. People get puppies and then look at me in amazement that the dog had an accident in the house. "I just took him outside and he came right back in and peed!" How should he know what's expected of him? Is he a full grown human being with a lifetime of experience? Of course not!

Expecting your puppy to know how to act is like expecting a baby not to use a diaper. It's impossible. In fact, a dog's brain cannot fully retain knowledge until he is three-and-a-half to four months old. So, if your dog is not "getting it" before that time, it is because he can't. He does not have the brainpower or development time to understand. Be patient!

I have seen so many dog parents put a leash on an eight-week-old puppy and immediately expect the puppy to go walking down the street with perfect manners. Why should he? How should he know what a leash is for? He's never read about leashes in a book or seen them on T.V.

It's amazing how much we expect of our dogs right away. I think it comes from having seen perfectly behaved dogs before. We watch T.V. shows or movies where dogs can do incredible things. Their manners are perfect or they're just so cute. We see people walking their dog on a leash with perfect behavior. We don't see the hours of work that went into achieving that behavior.

The saddest stories are when people adopt a dog without really thinking about it. They have an impulse or see a cute puppy and immediately take him home. As soon as the dog has an accident or chews something up, they immediately want to get rid of the dog. They yell and scream and lose their tempers over something the dog can't help. Millions of unwanted dogs each year go through these horrible experiences. Through no fault of their own, they receive abuse and abandonment simply for following their nature.

This is part of the reason I teach and write about dogs. I feel that if I can help one person to understand their dog more clearly, they will carry that knowledge throughout their life. They will look at every dog differently, from that point forward. Hopefully, they will spread this knowledge to the people in their lives. If we just took a little bit of time to understand our dogs, their behavior wouldn't seem so strange to us.

UNINTENDED MESSAGES

All day long, as we go about our lives, we are sending messages about ourselves. Most of the time, we aren't even consciously aware of the story we are telling with our bodies. The way we walk, talk, carry ourselves and the expressions on our face all combine to speak volumes about us.

When you walk down the street...

Do you slouch?

Do you stand up straight?

Do you look at the ground?

Do you look straight ahead?

You may not know it, but people see these things and make both conscious and unconscious judgments about you. In a split second, we decide whether a person is confident, insecure, weak, strong, nice, not so nice and a thousand other things. Your dog is doing the same thing.

In an even more pure and direct way than humans, an animal will "read" you. They really couldn't care less about the words you are saying. They want to know who you are. What is this person all about who is standing in front of me? Just like us, they make a snap judgment and react.

This is why the first few seconds of any encounter with a dog are the most crucial. A dog first decides what you're about and then moves onto the next step, which is how to treat you. How you make your first approach has a lasting impression and will affect how you relate to each dog you meet.

Many people enter the home of a friend who has a dog and right away, they begin gushing with affection. "Oh, what a cute puppy!" They bend down and pet the dog and coo and baby talk and fawn all over the dog. Humans think this is just wonderful and many dogs come to accept this behavior, over time. They grow to accept that this is how people like to behave and how they share love and affection. However, it's certainly not how dogs greet each other.

Think about this way of meeting from a dog's point of view. The doorbell rings, as it has many times before. This immediately means a break in the dog's routine. Somebody is here! That can be exciting, fearful, unnerving, wonderful or scary. It all depends on the experiences the dog has had with people coming to the house. Whatever has happened in the dog's past, he will react accordingly. Maybe he barks, lunges, maybe he's calm and passive, maybe he's somewhere in between.

Then, the door opens. Let's say you have the kind of dog that is excited and happy to see guests. He's barking, wagging his tail and running up to greet your guest. Maybe he jumps on them. Your guest, being a dog lover, immediately bends down or crouches and starts speaking in a loving, high-pitched tone of voice. They put their hands all over the dog's head and body and shower him with affection. He may like this and that's fine. If it doesn't bother you and the dog is well behaved, maybe it's not a problem worth addressing. However, if you have behavioral challenges, this is an excellent place to start changing our behavior.

Think of it from your dog's angle. Here comes this new person. The first thing that happens is he does is dominate them with excitement. In return, they bend down and show with their body language that they are submitting to his authority. They are, in essence, saying, "I'm no threat. You're the king of this house. I surrender to your leadership." Then, they put their hands all over the dog, in his face and all over his head and body.

How would you like it if, within the first few seconds of meeting someone, they squealed with excitement, ran their fingers through your hair and rubbed your belly?

I don't think you'd have a very positive response! You might like these things in the right time and place. However, the first few seconds of an encounter with someone are not the time or place.

Let's look at this encounter in a completely different way. Have you watched dogs when they meet each other? They rarely make a sound at all. They approach each other, side by side, and begin sniffing. If it is a good, peaceful first encounter, they begin sniffing the rear of the other dog. Of course, I would never suggest you have to do that!

The main thing we want to imitate is the quiet, calm energy of the meeting. We want to remain quiet and relatively calm, the way dogs do. Second, they don't stare each other directly in the eye or lunge at each other face to face. This is considered confrontational in the dog world and, in some cases, can trigger a fight. Therefore, forcing yourself on a dog from the front is going against nature.

I suggest that when you first meet a dog, remain calm, quiet and relaxed. Don't look the dog in the eye. In fact, just ignore the dog. This is usually the hardest thing in the world for people to do. We have been taught since childhood that it is rude to ignore someone when we meet them. I assure you, your dog does not see it that way at all. Often, to a dog, rude equals authority. They interpret indifference as a sort of inner strength and calm. They don't think it's rude to ignore them. In fact, you're giving them the opportunity to discover you on their own, at their own pace, without crowding or intimidating them.

When we are quiet and calm and don't force ourselves into the dog's space, he has a chance to meet us, first through his sense of smell. Since this is his primary sense, he is reading us in the most natural way possible. He gets an idea of who we are and what we are about in a calm, comfortable way. If we are relaxed and calm during this process, then the dog decides that that this is the kind of person we are.

Once the initial moment has passed and the dog has moved on from exploring someone new, that's when they start to interact. Usually, they want to initiate play or affection. You've seen dogs do this little dance when they meet. They sniff, they explore, and they check each other out. As long as neither is a threat or a negative encounter happens, they move into developing the next phase of their friendship.

When we take just a few seconds to behave in a neutral way, we send a message to the dog that we are relaxed and strong. We know who we are and we know what we're about. It changes the way the rest of our time together goes. The dog respects us and looks at us as an authority figure. Then, when we move into a moment of affection, the message is… "Strong, but loving. Authoritative, but fair. In control, but not overbearing." This, to a dog, is the type of person they are drawn to follow. This is the type of person they adore. It will give you a beautiful foundation to build on.

It took me a long time to discover this simple truth about dogs. I wasn't aware of these kinds of rituals for quite a while. Once I did start to understand how important these rituals are to them, I also realized how important they were in my life with humans.

As we go through our day and live our lives, most of us aren't thinking about how we're holding ourselves. We don't dwell on the subconscious messages we send to others with our posture and our tone of voice. However, now that you are thinking about it, think about your own way of interacting.

When I started changing the way I carried myself around dogs, without realizing it, I began changing the way I carried myself in general. I didn't see, for example, that I'd been slouching. My posture was horrible! My shoulders slumped and my neck jutted out and I tended to walk sort of aimlessly. I started looking in the mirror and making some simple adjustments in the way I carried myself. More importantly, though, I started standing differently around dogs. It was like a miracle!

At first this might sound dramatic. I guarantee, the results *were* dramatic! When I stood tall and walked into room like I owned it, any dog there treated me differently. This simple act changed my whole way of behaving in general. I began carrying this principle into my life. Just by changing my posture and a few body movements, I noticed people were treating me differently.

Your dog doesn't reason and think through each moment. He doesn't ask himself why he is reacting to you the way he is. He is simply following his instinct. People do exactly the same thing. They aren't always analyzing why they are drawn to you. They don't always know why they get a good feeling about you or want to be around you. Sometimes the message is subtle and it hits them subconsciously.

I started experimenting. I would walk into a store or restaurant, stand a little straighter, smile more confidently and walk a little bit like I owned the place. I began getting quicker attention, help in stores, faster service in restaurants and better results in personal encounters. It started affecting my business and the way others treated me. All of this happened because of the simple act of adjusting my body language. And I learned this from dogs.

Dogs are not capable of lying. They can't deceive you. Therefore, they treat you exactly the way they see you. They will react according to the person you are presenting. Try changing your way of carrying yourself around a few dogs. Notice the difference. I believe you'll start to carry this into your own life. Even if it's subconscious, if you're anything like me, you won't be able to help but adjust your way of being. The results are significant.

VOICE

I learned a long time ago to get to the point with dogs. They don't use pronouns and adverbs and adjectives. We need to get to the heart of how they communicate. One of the hardest things for many of us to accept is that our dogs are animals. They are not human. We project human qualities onto them and make them our babies. I am just as guilty as anyone else of making this mistake. However, I try to catch myself and create a balance between what makes me feel good and what is good for them.

Animals don't beat around the bush. They communicate a specific idea with any and all means other than words. They don't have words in their world! Therefore, why should they understand our sentences and paragraphs? If you want to give your dog one of the greatest gifts he can receive, learn a little bit of his language.

How would you make a point if you couldn't rely on words?

I am always amazed when I watch dogs at how accurately they communicate. With their bodies, tone of voice and simple touches, the whole idea gets across. They read the truth of who you are and they accept what you present to them beyond concepts and words.

In fact, their brains don't reason in that way. They don't take roundabout ways to get to the heart of what they are trying to communicate. They are all about getting to the point.

Your voice is a very powerful tool in communicating with your dog. However, it's not about the words. Over time, they do learn an incredible list of words from us. They have to, living in our world. In fact, I think it's a miracle of nature that they can do this at all. They don't have a speech center in their brain!

Dogs primarily rely on the tone of our voice to convey a message. One low, short, sharp bark, for example, means stop what you're doing. I'm in control. When we use this type of "bark" associated with our word, we are cutting to the heart of the way a dog would correct or command another dog.

Adding words or paragraphs simply dilutes the message. Your dog would appreciate it if you would get to the point. However, when we are showing affection, I believe that is the time we can extend the conversation. Dogs often use whines or coos or higher pitched sounds to show excitement, happiness and simply being thrilled. If you like the state of mind your dog is in, that's the time to use the baby talk.

A dog's mind is associative. That means he associates what is going on with his inner experience. In other words, if you are giving affection and sharing pleasure, he will associate what he is doing with that affection. So, reserve the baby talk and love speak for times when you want your dog to feel rewarded for the state of mind he is in. You never want to try to calm your dog or bring him out of an aggressive or panicked state of mind with affection. It will only serve to reinforce those states of mind.

There is a subtle difference between calm tones of voice and affectionate tones. A calm, in control, rational sounding voice commands authority. A high-pitched, loving, baby talk voice creates excitement or sometimes, the opposite result we are trying to achieve. Try not to control your dog's behavior with excited, squealing tones of voice.

The only exception to this rule is very young puppies. We want them to be excited about learning and thrilled about training. When you want to motivate a puppy, there is nothing better than a treat and an excited tone of voice. Just like a baby, though, there comes a time when we shift from baby talk to adult talk.

We don't talk to a teenager with the same tone of voice we talk to an infant. Therefore, as your dog matures, you will, hopefully, find yourself shifting into a voice that is more balanced and rational. As we start to create a contrast in our voice that is very clear, we provide a form of communication the dog can get his mind around.

When a dog is doing well, our tone is soft, sweet, even baby talk.

When our dog is doing something unwanted, our voice is sharp, low and quick.

This way the dog can associate the clearly different tones with two different kinds of behavior. Keep it black and white, right or wrong, good or bad. The more "sing-songy" or complicated the sentences and tones, rising and falling, the harder it is for our dog to follow what point we are trying to make.

Remember, your dog is wired in a completely different way than you are. Without human complexity, the ability to reason and think in our complicated way, how should your dog know what you want from him? Keep it simple!

For some reason, we seem to find it easier to accept that a baby or a toddler isn't ready for big expectations. However, we get a puppy or a rescue dog and expect huge results instantly. I find life so much easier when I lower my expectations for my dog, especially when they are new to my house. Then, with every miraculous new behavior, each amazing new trick, I am overjoyed! I think this way of thinking is a beautiful foundation for the beginning of a wonderful relationship with our dog.

LIFE

If you've ever had a relationship with a dog, you know how it can change you. You know that unspoken connection that happens when your dog's eyes look into yours. You've felt that deep love that is truly unconditional. Your dog has never had to do anything to make you love them. You have never had to do anything to earn love back from your dog. Your dog has never had to explain that love to you or tell you anything at all, verbally. Yet, you have an understanding.

If you can carry one lesson from this book into your life, it is how to love unconditionally.

A dog's love is quiet, non-verbal and peaceful. It's given and shown with very little effort and no self-doubt. A dog dives into life with great enthusiasm and joy. Their life is shorter than ours, so they get right to the point. They are who they appear to be. They don't deceive and can't lie. They will follow their leader into any kind of situation if they are mutually loved and respected. They are loyal to the end.

A dog gives his trust freely, as long as you don't betray it. You can depend on your dog unconditionally. There is nothing in the world like a relationship between a dog and his guardian. Respect that.

Treat your dog with the dignity and adoration he deserves. They ask very little in return for giving you their whole lives. If we understand them just a little bit better, we can open up volumes within ourselves. We are better people for having known our dogs.

Made in the USA
Lexington, KY
30 June 2019